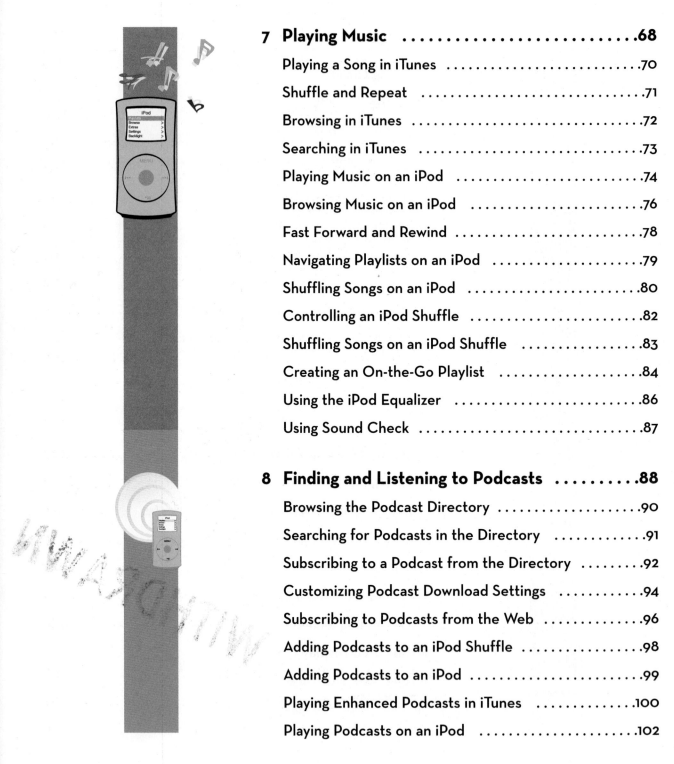

EASY iPOD® AND iTUNES®

International Standard Book Number: 0-7897-3544-x

Library of Congress Catalog Card Number: 2005938384

Printed in the United States of America

First Printing: April 2006

09   08   07   06   4   3   2   1

U.K. International Standard Book Number: 0-7897-3567-9

First Printing: April 2006

09   08   07   06   4   3   2   1

TRADEMARKS

All terms mentioned in this book that are known to be trademarks or service marks have been appropriately capitalized. Que Publishing cannot attest to the accuracy of this information. Use of a term in this book should not be regarded as affecting the validity of any trademark or service mark.

iPod and iTunes are registered trademarks of Apple, Inc.

WARNING AND DISCLAIMER

BULK SALES

Que Publishing offers excellent discounts on this book when ordered in quantity for bulk purchases or special sales. For more information, please contact

U.S. Corporate and Government Sales

1-800-382-3419

corpsales@pearsontechgroup.com

For sales outside the United States, please contact

International Sales

international@pearsoned.com

Associate Publisher
Greg Wiegand

Acquisitions Editor
Laura Norman

Development Editor
Laura Norman

Managing Editor
Charlotte Clapp

Project Editor
Tonya Simpson

Production Editor
Heather Wilkins

Indexer
Aaron Black

Technical Editor
Kate Binder

Publishing Coordinator
Sharry Lee Gregory

Interior Designer
Anne Jones

Cover Designer
Anne Jones

Page Layout
Michelle Mitchell

ABOUT THE AUTHOR

Shelly Brisbin has written about technology for 18 years. She is the author of 12 books, including *The MacAddict Guide to Living the iLife, Build Your Own Wi-Fi Network, Adobe GoLive 6 for Macintosh and Windows Visual QuickStart Guide,* and *Mac Answers: Certified Tech Support.* She has also written hundreds of articles for magazines including *MacAddict, Macworld, MacWeek, NetProfessional, The Net, NewMedia, WebTechniques,* and *SunWorld.* Shelly produces and hosts three podcasts, including the acclaimed personal blog and tech commentary show, Shelly's Podcast.

Her most recent day job was managing editor/technology at Powered, Inc. in Austin, Texas. Previously, she spent four-and-a-half years as networking editor for *MacUser* magazine. Shelly has also worked as a webmaster, system administrator, and consultant. In her free time, she manages a music-related website and mailing list.

DEDICATION

For my father, Windel Brisbin.

ACKNOWLEDGMENTS

Thanks to the Que team: Laura Norman, tech editor Kate Binder, project editor Tonya Simpson, and production editor Heather Wilkins.

I had the help of several vendors who provided iPod accessories and photos for this book. Thanks to Sam Levin (Griffin Technologies), Kristin Pribble (Otterbox), Jacqueline Romulo (Belkin), Mike Talmadge (ThroughOut), and Jaime Schopflin (Apple Computer).

Thanks as always to my husband, Frank, who does not own an iPod. He has promised to read this book anyway.

WE WANT TO HEAR FROM YOU!

As the reader of this book, *you* are our most important critic and commentator. We value your opinion and want to know what we're doing right, what we could do better, what areas you'd like to see us publish in, and any other words of wisdom you're willing to pass our way.

As an associate publisher for Que Publishing, I welcome your comments. You can email or write me directly to let me know what you did or didn't like about this book—as well as what we can do to make our books better.

Please note that I cannot help you with technical problems related to the topic of this book. We do have a User Services group, however, where I will forward specific technical questions related to the book.

When you write, please be sure to include this book's title and author as well as your name, email address, and phone number. I will carefully review your comments and share them with the author and editors who worked on the book.

Email: feedback@quepublishing.com

Mail: Greg Wiegand
            Associate Publisher
            Que Publishing
            800 East 96th Street
            Indianapolis, IN 46240 USA

For more information about this book or another Que Publishing title, visit our website at www.quepublishing.com. Type the ISBN (excluding hyphens) or the title of a book in the Search field to find the page you're looking for.

IT'S AS EASY AS 1-2-3

Each part of this book is made up of a series of short, instructional lessons, designed to help you understand basic information.

1 Each step is fully illustrated to show you how it looks onscreen.

2 Each task includes a series of quick, easy steps designed to guide you through the procedure.

3 Items that you select or click in menus, dialog boxes, tabs, and windows are shown in **bold**.

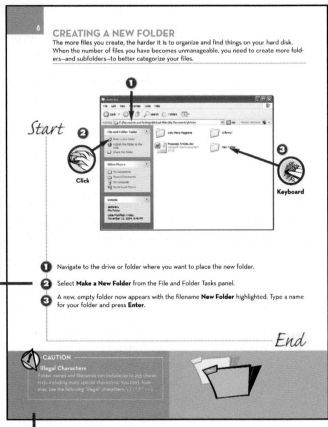

Start

8 CREATING A NEW FOLDER
The more files you create, the harder it is to organize and find things on your hard disk. When the number of files you have becomes unmanageable, you need to create more folders—and subfolders—to better categorize your files.

1 Navigate to the drive or folder where you want to place the new folder.

2 Select **Make a New Folder** from the File and Folder Tasks panel.

3 A new, empty folder now appears with the filename **New Folder** highlighted. Type a name for your folder and press **Enter**.

End

CAUTION
Illegal Characters
Folder names and filenames can include up to 255 characters—including many special characters. You can't, however, use the following "illegal" characters: \ / : * ? " < > |

Drag

Click

How to Drag:
Point to the starting place or object. Hold down the mouse button (right or left per instructions), move the mouse to the new location, then release the button.

Tips, notes and cautions give you a heads-up for any extra information you may need while working through the task.

Click:
Click the left mouse button once.

Keyboard

Click & Type:
Click once where indicated and begin typing to enter your text or data.

Selection:
Highlights the area onscreen discussed in the step or task.

Double-click:
Click the left mouse button twice in rapid succession.

Right-click:
Click the right mouse button once.

Pointer Arrow:
Highlights an item on the screen you need to point to or focus on in the step or task.

INTRODUCTION TO *EASY iPOD AND iTUNES*

Part of the iPod's beauty is its simplicity—just add music and start rocking. But sometimes, when computers are involved, things can get a little confusing. Whether you're instantly at ease with gadgets or feel a little intimidated, *Easy iPod and iTunes* gives you a crash course in setting up, filling, and using your iPod, along with lots of help working with iTunes.

Easy iPod and iTunes consists of step-by-step tasks that walk you through every step on the road to getting iPod and iTunes up and running. Every task in the book is described in words and pictures, and each page features tips that point out useful features or alternate ways to do the tasks described.

To help you find the information you need, *Easy iPod and iTunes* is organized into 17 parts.

Parts 1–3 introduce you to the iPod and then show you how to connect it to your computer and get music downloaded or copied into iTunes. In Parts 4–6 you learn how to get around iTunes, including the iTunes Music Store, where you can find everything from your favorite tunes to audiobooks to the latest movie trailers that you can download using iTunes. After you've downloaded all your favorites to iTunes, you'll work on organizing and managing all that stuff with playlists and then learn how to move them over to your iPod.

Parts 7–10 get into the heart of why you got an iPod in the first place. You learn all the tips and tricks for listening to music on your iPod, as well as finding podcasts, audiobooks, and videos to expand your audio horizons. Parts 11 and 12 show you how to view photos on your iPod and how to use your iPod as a hard disk or PDA. In Parts 13 and 14 you find tasks to assist you with managing your iTunes library as well as doing some interesting things with your downloaded music, such as adding album artwork and lyrics.

In Part 15 you'll focus on additional portability options. You learn how to burn CDs and DVDs using iTunes and how to print disk inserts. Part 16 provides some advanced tasks such as sharing your iTunes library and streaming music wirelessly. In the final part, Part 17, you look at how to take care of your iPod. It's your investment and you need to know how to troubleshoot problems should they arise. Last, an appendix describes a brief selection of accessories for customizing your iPod or adding functionality, such as docks, travel accessories, and so on.

Whether using cool gadgets such as the iPod is second nature to you or a new challenge, I know you will find many helpful, step-by-step explanations and many useful tips for getting the most out of your music and your music player.

GETTING TO KNOW THE iPOD

This chapter assumes that your iPod is brand-new, and that you're eager to start using it. Later chapters offer information for folks who might have been using an iPod and iTunes software for awhile. But for now, I'm talking just to the iPod newbies.

I'll bet you knew what an iPod looked like even before you purchased one. They're everywhere these days; the familiar white or black rectangle encased in a skin, or a snazzy case, and the signature white earbuds. And you know that the iPod's job is to play your music. In this part, you literally go inside the iPod box and are introduced to the device, its accessories, and how you and your computer will interact with it.

Apple makes three kinds of iPods: the iPod shuffle; iPod nano; and iPod, sometimes called the fifth generation iPod. Each model comes in two sizes. In this case, size refers not to the iPod's physical dimensions, but its storage capacity. Other iPod models have come and gone, including the colorful iPod mini, which has been replaced by the nano. Although they aren't described in detail, much of what you read throughout this book still applies to the iPod mini as well as to all the other first through fourth generation iPods.

The nano and fifth generation iPod each support photos. You can play slideshows or connect the iPod to your television. Speaking of TV, the fifth generation iPod is the first to support video; you can play MPEG-4 or H.264 video files. To see photos or video on a television, you'll need to buy an optional cable from Apple.

iPOD MODELS

iPod

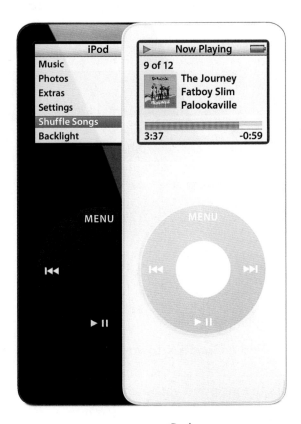

iPod nano

iPod shuffle

iPOD

The flagship product in the iPod line is simply called the iPod. Available with 30GB or 60GB of storage space (that translates to 7500 or 15,000 songs), the iPod has a color display and is controlled by a click wheel. They come in black or white. In addition to music, iPod stores and displays videos, photos and notes, and even includes a few games. You can connect the iPod to a stereo system in your home or car, a pair of speakers, or even a television (for video or photo display).

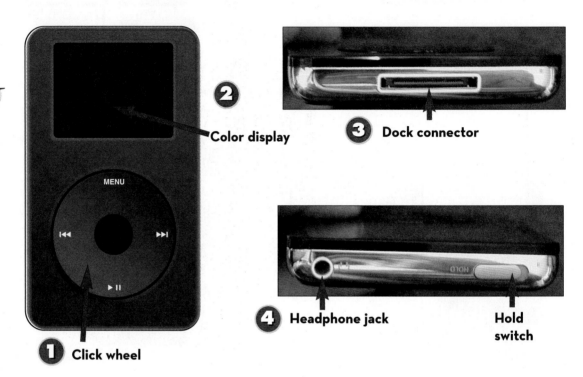

Start

Color display

②

③ **Dock connector**

④ **Headphone jack**

Hold switch

① **Click wheel**

① The **click wheel** controls playback and other features of the iPod.

② All current iPods include a **color display**, except for the shuffle.

③ The **dock connector port** on the bottom of the iPod connects it to your computer, a dock, or a charger.

④ The **headphone jack** on top of the iPod accepts the included earbud headphones (or any pair with a standard 1/8-inch RCA connector), or one of a variety of remotes.

End

─ NOTE ─

Hold Everything

The hold switch on the top of the iPod locks the device so that accidentally pressing a button does not activate the iPod. Turn hold off to use the iPod's click wheel and button.

iPOD NANO

It's tiny and it looks really cool. The iPod nano is a Flash-based player with a color display and room for 1GB (240 songs), 2GB (500 songs), or 4GB (1,000 songs). Flash players store files on an internal chip rather than a mechanical hard drive, making them more durable than hard drive–based iPods. The nano comes in black or white.

Start

1 Click wheel

2 Dock connector   **2** Headphone jack

1 Like its larger cousin, the nano is operated with a **click wheel** and a menu-based display.

2 There's a standard **dock connector**, too, and a **headphone jack** on the bottom.

End

TIP
No FireWire
The fifth generation iPod and iPod nano dock connectors support the same cables and docks as older iPods. But you'll need the included USB 2 cable to sync with these models because they do not support FireWire.

NOTE
Dock Adapter
The nano's dock connector supports standard iPod accessories, but because the nano is so thin, it won't stand up when inserted into many speaker docks. Apple includes a dock adapter to keep the nano upright.

iPOD SHUFFLE

The little white strip of plastic looks like no other iPod, but it has that Apple magic, just like the big guys. 512MB and 1GB models give you 120 or 240 songs, loaded randomly when you sync the shuffle to your computer.

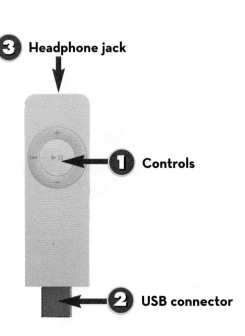

3 Headphone jack

1 Controls

2 USB connector

Start

End

1 There's no display, just controls you use to move through your shuffled music.

2 Beneath a cap on the bottom of the shuffle is a **USB connector**.

3 Connect headphones to the top.

TIP

Adapt to It

The shuffle's USB connector fits directly into a USB port on your computer—no cable required. On the downside, space is tight on some laptops, and you might not have room to connect the shuffle because of its broad "shoulders," especially if other USB ports are in use. You can purchase a USB adapter cable (female on one end, male on the other) and plug the shuffle into the cable, which then connects easily to your computer.

WHAT'S IN THE BOX

Each iPod model comes with software and accessories. The CD includes Mac and PC versions of the iPod driver software, as well as iTunes.

Start

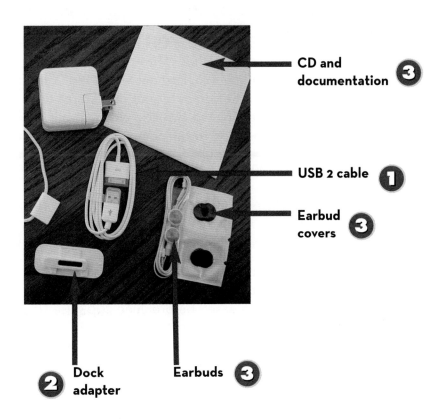

CD and documentation **3**

USB 2 cable **1**

Earbud covers **3**

2 Dock adapter

Earbuds **3**

1 Each iPod and iPod nano model comes with a **USB 2 cable**.

2 The iPod and iPod nano includes a **dock adapter** for use with dock connector iPod accessories.

3 You'll find a CD containing documentation and software, as well as a pair of those spiffy white **earbud headphones** in all iPod boxes.

End

 NOTE

Your Contents Might Vary

Apple has a habit of changing the contents of its iPod packages, usually to reduce the retail price of the player. For example, bigger iPods used to come with remote controls—way, way back when you got a carrying case, too. Be sure you know what's in the box before you take your new iPod home. You might want to get accessories while you're still in the store, or before finalizing your order when shopping online.

CONNECTING YOUR iPOD TO A MAC OR PC

Before you can begin rocking out with your iPod, you need to introduce it to your computer. The computer not only stores the songs that you'll copy to the iPod, but connecting the two also charges your iPod's battery. The first time you connect the iPod to the computer, you also install software.

Your iPod connects to your PC or Mac via USB 2. In the case of the iPod and iPod nano, you use a cable called a *dock connector* with a special connector on one end. The iPod end is thinner and wider than other USB connectors. The other end of the cable is a standard USB connector. The iPod shuffle needs no cable: You plug it directly into your computer's USB port.

If you have an old computer that has only USB 1 (the two ports look identical), you can connect and use your iPod, but you'll notice that copying files is very slow. No Macs released before June 2003 use USB 2, and some more recent Macs offer only USB 1. Similarly, if you connect an iPod to a PC's USB 1 port on a computer that has USB 2, Windows tells you that you can get better performance by connecting to the USB 2 port.

Connecting any iPod model to your computer charges the iPod's battery. Before you connect the iPod, install the software from the CD that came with the iPod.

CONNECT YOUR iPOD TO YOUR COMPUTER

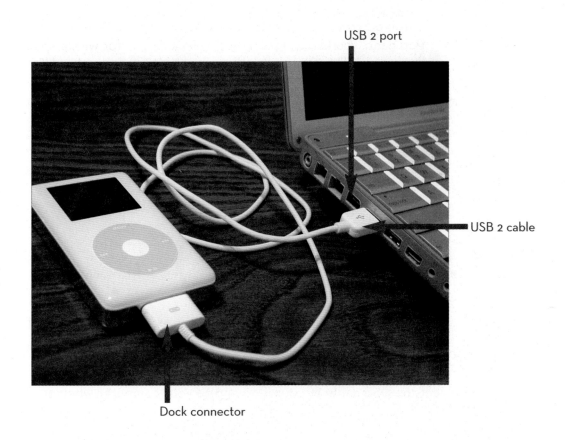

USB 2 port

USB 2 cable

Dock connector

INSTALLING iPOD SOFTWARE ON A PC

The CD supplied with your iPod contains software that supports all iPod models, as well as iTunes software for PCs and Macs (though Mac OS X users already have a copy installed with their system software). After you've installed iPod and iTunes software on your computer, you'll update your iPod's software and begin working with iTunes. The iPod installer begins the iPod setup process and adds a copy of iTunes to your system if it isn't already installed.

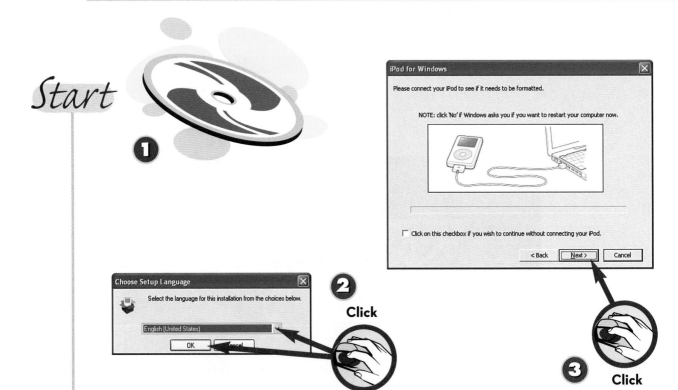

Start

① Click

② Click

③ Click

① With the iPod nearby but not connected to the PC, insert the iPod CD into your drive.

② Choose a language from the drop-down menu when asked, and click **OK** to begin following the wizard's instructions.

③ Connect the USB cable to your iPod and to your computer when asked. (If you have an iPod shuffle, remove the cap from the shuffle and insert it into a USB port on your computer.) Wait for the PC to scan the iPod. The iPod is formatted if it isn't empty; otherwise you'll be asked to click **Next** to complete the setup process.

Continued

 — **NOTE**

Just the Software

If you check the **Click on the Checkbox If You Wish to Continue Without Connecting Your iPod** option, you can install iPod software on the computer only. You can always update your iPod's contents at a later time.

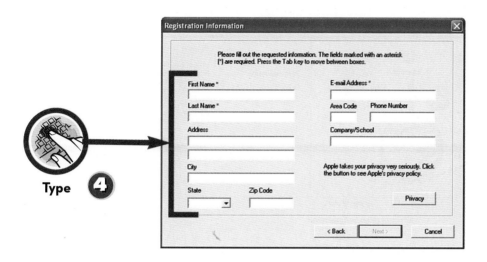

Registration Information

Please fill out the requested information. The fields marked with an asterisk (*) are required. Press the Tab key to move between boxes.

First Name *

Last Name *

Address

City

State   Zip Code

E-mail Address *

Area Code   Phone Number

Company/School

Apple takes your privacy very seriously. Click the button to see Apple's privacy policy.

Privacy

< Back   Next >   Cancel

Type **4**

4 Enter the iPod's serial number, click **Next**, and enter your registration information when asked. The serial number is on the back of the iPod or on the bar code tag on the box. Click **Next**.

5 Continue following the wizard's steps to install iTunes. If you are connected to the Internet and a newer version of iTunes is available, you can download and install it.

End

NOTE

To Register or Not

Registering your iPod lets Apple know that you have purchased it and might make it easier to obtain service and repair, if necessary. You might choose not to register if you are adamant about keeping your name off mailing lists, but otherwise, registering is a great way to ensure that your iPod is protected while under warranty.

INSTALLING iPOD SOFTWARE ON A MAC

Mac OS X comes preloaded with a copy of iTunes and software to support the iPod. That software is likely to be out-of-date, however, and might not even support the brand-new iPod you've just opened. You should always install iPod software from the disc that came with the iPod.

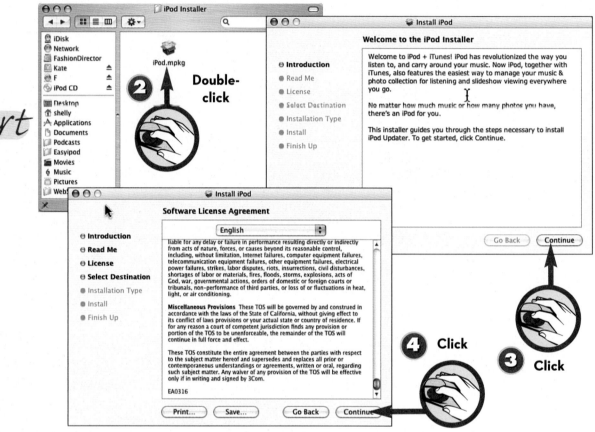

1 Insert the iPod Software CD into your drive.

2 Open the iPod installer folder and double-click the **iPod.mpkg** file.

3 Click **Continue** to begin installation.

4 Read the Before You Install screen and the license agreement. Click **Continue** after each screen.

Continued

TIP
iTunes Inside

All Macs ship with a copy of iTunes installed. You can re-install it along with the iPod software if iTunes is no longer on your Mac, but chances are you won't need to do so.

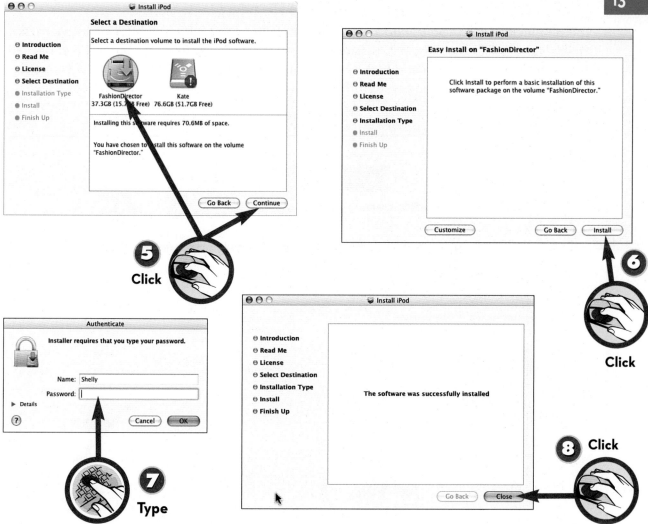

5 Click a disk to choose where to install the iPod software, and click **Continue**.

6 Click **Install** to begin copying software to your hard drive.

7 Enter your Mac's administrator password to authorize and initiate installation.

8 Click **Close** to complete installation.

End

NOTE

The Two-Step

Plugging your iPod into the computer is not a part of the Mac OS X installation process, as it is in Windows. After software is installed, you can connect the iPod at any time and begin setting it up with iTunes.

UPDATING SOFTWARE ON THE MAC

The disc included with your iPod contains a recent version of iPod and iTunes software, but there's a possibility that Apple has issued an update since that disc was burned and packed. iPod software updates can add features to your iPod or provide support for new versions of your computer's operating system. They might also fix bugs in previous versions. New iTunes versions might also squash bugs or add important new features. It's almost always a good idea to update your software. You'll need to be connected to the Internet to run these updates.

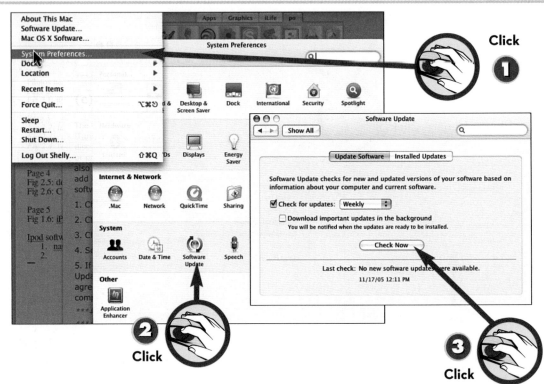

Click **1**

Click **2**

Click **3**

1 Choose **Apple, System Preferences**.

2 Click the **Software Update** button.

3 Click **Check Now** to begin looking for updates from Apple. If new software is available, you see a list of available updates. Click **Install** to add them.

End

TIP
Schedule Updates
Software Update lets you know when new versions of all Apple software installed on your Mac have been updated. Just check the **Check for Updates** check box and choose an interval from the menu.

CHARGING YOUR iPOD

All iPod models contain a rechargeable lithium battery. iPods with screens have a battery strength indicator in the upper-right corner that gives you a reasonable approximation of how much battery life is left in the current charge.

When an iPod is connected to the computer, its battery is charged until it's full. If you have a power adapter (standard iPods come with them and you can buy one for your iPod nano), you can also connect directly to an AC adapter.

Start

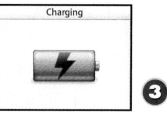

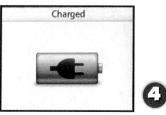

1 Connect your iPod to a computer or to a wall outlet with an AC adapter.

2 A standard iPod or iPod nano displays the **Don't Disconnect** symbol when the iPod is mounted in iTunes.

3 When the iPod is connected to the computer but not mounted in iTunes, you see the Charging indicator.

4 When the iPod is fully charged, you see **Charged** on the screen.

End

NOTE

How Long Should You Charge?

Different iPod models require different amounts of time to charge and offer different amounts of battery life. Apple often improves battery performance when new iPod models are released. For reference, the standard iPod used to prepare this book was 80% charged after one hour and fully charged after four hours. The iPod nano reached 80% charge after one and one-half hours and full charge after three hours. An iPod shuffle requires two hours for an 80% charge, four for full charge.

SETTING UP YOUR iPOD

With both iPod software and iTunes installed, you're ready to set up your iPod to work with your computer. To copy music and other audio from your computer to your iPod, you must decide how often to synchronize the computer and the iPod, or whether to do it at all. You can also give your iPod a name and choose whether to use it as both a music player and a disk drive on your computer.

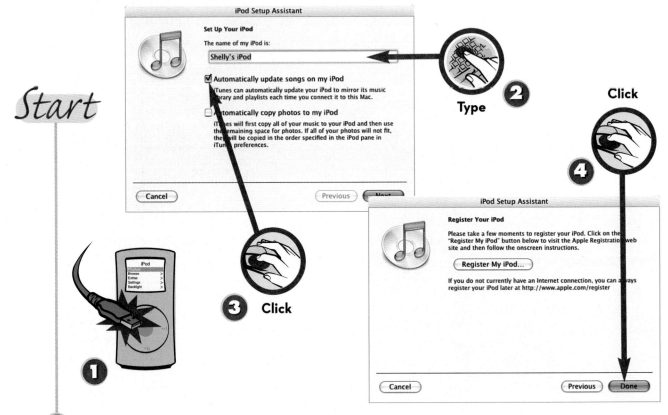

Start

Type ② **Click**

④

Click ③

①

① Connect the iPod to your computer.

② When the setup assistant (Mac OS) or wizard (Windows) opens, type a name for your iPod.

③ Click **Automatically Update Songs on My iPod** to have iTunes fill your iPod or iPod nano automatically. On an iPod shuffle iTunes adds a random selection of songs. Click **Next**.

④ If you haven't already sent information to Apple and want to do so, click **Register My iPod**. If you've already registered, click **Done**.

Continued

TIP

Change Is OK

If you decide to automatically sync your music library with your iPod and change your mind later, you can make the change in iTunes Preferences. Learn more about setting these preferences in Part 6, "Setting Up Your iPod."

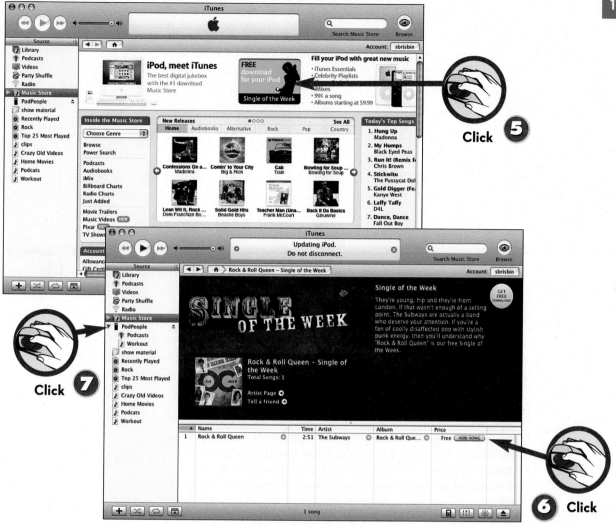

5 iTunes switches to the Music Store when the iPod setup is complete. At this writing, new iPod owners can download a free Single of the Week from the Music Store the first time they connect the iPod. Click the banner to access this offer.

6 Click **Add Song** (if you're using a Music Store shopping cart) and download the free song to your computer.

7 The iPod appears in the iTunes source pane. If playlists have been added, click the expansion triangle to see them, and click a playlist to see its contents.

End

ADDING MUSIC TO YOUR iTUNES LIBRARY

The first step to getting music on your iPod is to add it to your computer's iTunes library. The library is both a folder hierarchy where your files are stored and a database that keeps your music files organized so you can find it or copy it to your iPod. The library accepts audio files in all of the formats supported by your iPod. You can also add movies and PDF files, which you'll learn about in Parts 9, "Watching Video in iTunes and on Your iPod," and 14, "Adding Lyrics and Artwork to Your Music Library."

You can bring audio files into your iTunes library from a wide variety of sources: audio CDs, files from your computer or downloaded from the Web, or songs you buy from the iTunes Music Store. You can add files in a number of audio formats, including MP3, WAV, Apple Lossless, and AAC. You can also convert files from an uncompressed (big file) format to a compressed (smaller file) format so more music fits on your iPod. That's called *encoding*.

In this part, I show you many ways to bring music into iTunes. Although none of these methods are prohibited by copyright laws in the United States, you should familiarize yourself with laws that govern when music can be copied to your computer. For example, you can rip a CD you own to your Mac or PC, but it is illegal to copy a friend's CD.

iTUNES IMPORTING

SETTING MUSIC IMPORTING PREFERENCES

When you add music to your iTunes library, the files are copied to your computer in the iTunes folder. Files are typically converted from their original uncompressed format to a compressed format you can choose. You can also import compressed files, including MP3s. Before you import music from a CD or copy it from another source, take a few moments to set importing preferences in iTunes.

Click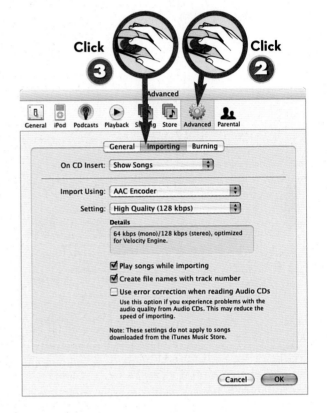

Click

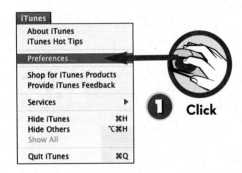

Click

Click

iTunes

About iTunes
iTunes Hot Tips

Preferences...

Shop for iTunes Products
Provide iTunes Feedback

Services ▶

Hide iTunes ⌘H
Hide Others ⌥⌘H
Show All

Quit iTunes ⌘Q

Advanced

General iPod Podcasts Playback Sharing Store Advanced Parental

General Importing Burning

On CD Insert: Show Songs

Import Using: AAC Encoder

Setting: High Quality (128 kbps)

Details
64 kbps (mono)/128 kbps (stereo), optimized for Velocity Engine.

☑ Play songs while importing
☑ Create file names with track number
☐ Use error correction when reading Audio CDs
Use this option if you experience problems with the audio quality from Audio CDs. This may reduce the speed of importing.

Note: These settings do not apply to songs downloaded from the iTunes Music Store.

Cancel   OK

1 **Mac user:** In iTunes, pull down the **iTunes** menu and choose **Preferences**.
Windows user: In iTunes, pull down the **Edit** menu and choose **Preferences**.

2 Click the **Advanced** button.

3 Click the **Importing** tab.

Continued

NOTE

Format Choices
AAC is the best compressed format available. If you plan to transfer imported files out of iTunes or play them on a non-iPod music player, you can import files as MP3s instead. AIFF and WAV are uncompressed formats that create very large files. AIFF is the format found on audio CDs; WAV is a standard Windows file format; and Apple Lossless is the company's high-quality, moderately compressed format.

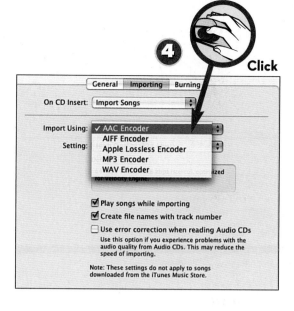

Click **4**

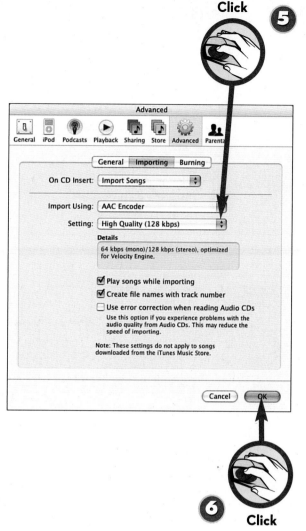

Click **5**

Click **6**

4 Choose **AAC Encoder** from the Import Using drop-down menu, if it isn't already selected. AAC is a compressed file format that's a higher quality than MP3.

5 Choose **High Quality** from the Setting menu if you intend to import music.

6 Click **OK** to close Preferences.

End

NOTE

Custom Encoding

Custom encoding settings are available from the **Settings** menu for each supported file format. These settings tweak the bit and sample rates, affecting the quality and size of the file (higher quality is better sounding but results in larger files). In most cases, you won't need to mess with these options.

IMPORTING MUSIC FROM A CD

iTunes can automatically import tracks from your audio CDs, making them available for playback on your computer or transfer to an iPod.

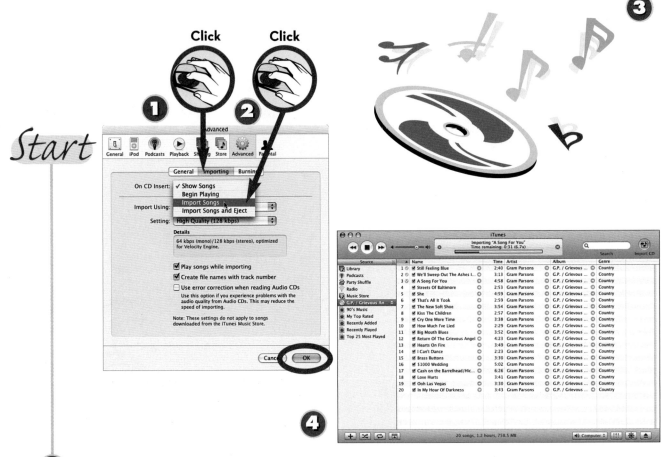

Start

Click   **Click**

1 In the **Advanced** tab of iTunes Preferences, click **Importing**.

2 Choose **Import Songs** from the On CD Insert menu, to tell iTunes to begin importing as soon as you insert the CD. Click **OK** to close.

3 Insert an audio CD into your drive.

4 iTunes contacts the Gracenote Media Database to obtain track information for your disc. Importing begins automatically. You hear an alert when the process is complete.

End

NOTE

Got Gracenote?

The Gracenote Media Database (formerly called CDDB) is an Internet repository of artist, track, and production information for thousands of songs and CDs. In most cases, iTunes is able to add Gracenote data to the CDs you import to your iTunes library. If the database doesn't return track information, you can add it manually. I show you how in Part 13, "Managing Your iTunes Library."

ADDING A FILE FROM YOUR COMPUTER

iTunes imports any supported audio file you copy from elsewhere on your computer. Formats include AIFF, WAV, MP3, AAC, and Apple Lossless. You can add the file by dragging it into the iTunes window or by using iTunes's menus.

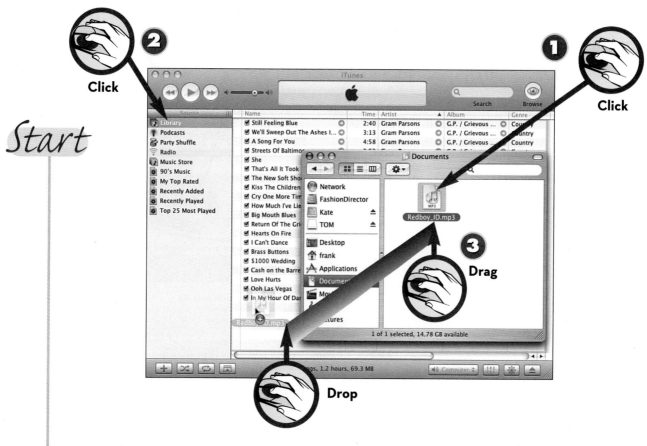

Start

1 In **Windows Explorer** (Windows) or the **Finder** (Mac), locate an audio file or a folder containing audio files.

2 Click the **iTunes Library** label to view it in the content pane.

3 Drag the file or folder and drop it in the iTunes window. iTunes imports the file(s).

End

TIP
Don't Be a Drag
There's an alternative way to add files to your iTunes library. In iTunes, choose **File**, **Add to Library**. Navigate to the file or folder you want to import, and click **Choose**. If you choose a folder, all compatible files within it are imported.

NOTE
ID3 Tags
Information, such as title and artist, about an audio file you add to iTunes is stored in ID3 tags. When you import an audio CD, the ID3 tag information is added to your file.

ADDING A FILE FROM THE INTERNET

Downloading audio files that are protected by copyright and available for sale without paying for them is illegal, but there are plenty of freely available songs, sound clips, and podcasts out there, free for the taking from websites.

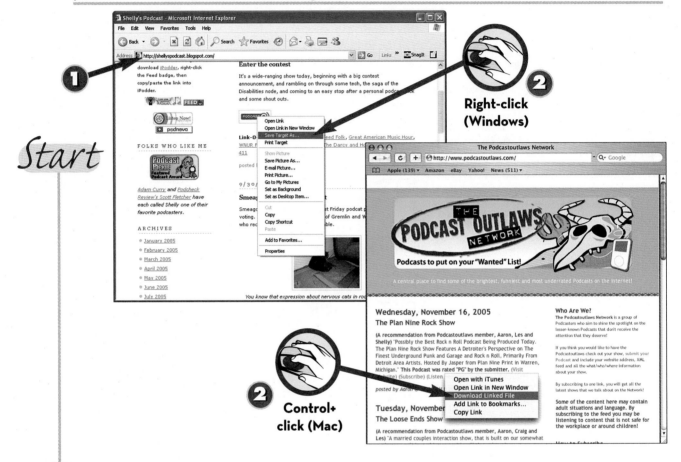

Start

Right-click
(Windows)

Control+
click (Mac)

1 Go to the web page containing the audio file you want to download.

2 Right-click (Windows) or Control+click (Mac) on the link and choose **Save Target As** (Internet Explorer), **Download Linked File** (Safari), or **Save Link As** (Firefox).

Continued

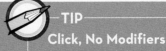

TIP
Click, No Modifiers
In most cases, clicking an audio file, rather than right-clicking or Control-clicking it, plays the file in your browser.

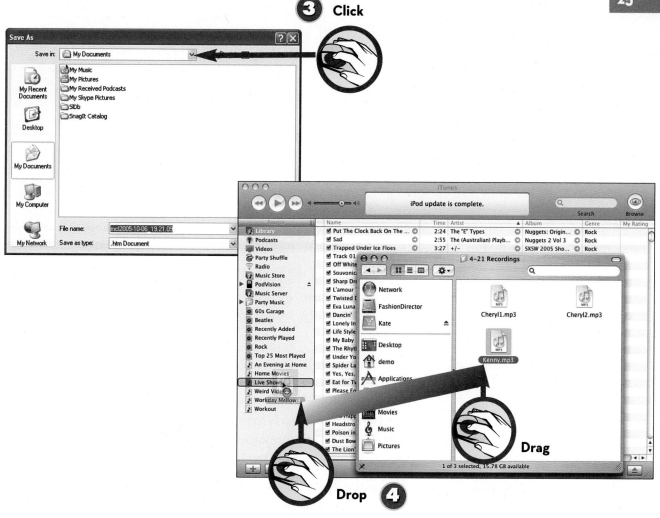

3 Click

4 Drag

Drop

3 Internet Explorer and Firefox ask you to choose a location on your hard drive; Safari begins downloading automatically.

4 When the download is complete, locate the file in Windows Explorer (Windows) or the Finder (Mac), and drag it into the iTunes window.

End

TIP

Safari Speaks iTunes

If you use Mac OS X and the Safari browser, you can skip a step by choosing **Open in iTunes** from the contextual menu when you ⌘+click the audio file.

THE iTUNES MUSIC STORE

With an account from the iTunes Music Store, you can buy and download music or audiobooks, and then add them to your computer or iPod. You can choose from thousands of individual songs for $.99 apiece, or buy a complete album for less than you would pay for a CD. After you purchase an item, it is automatically downloaded to your iTunes library.

The iTunes Music Store provides all sorts of ways to find the music you want. You can search by artist or song title, or browse by genre. You hear a 30-second preview of any song from the Music Store to be sure you like a tune before you buy it.

You can also buy videos—mostly television shows as I write this—and music videos. The TV episodes go for $1.99 an episode, as do most music videos. It's very likely that Apple will add more video content, now that the iPod can play it, and you should soon be able to search for the artists and shows you want to see. Watching videos in iTunes and on your iPod is covered thoroughly in Part 9, "Watching Video in iTunes and on Your iPod."

Audiobooks are also available at the Music Store. Through a partnership with Audible, as well as deals it has made on its own, Apple offers thousands of books, whose prices vary widely. Learn more about audiobooks at the Music Store in Part 10, "Listening to Audiobooks."

THE iTUNES MUSIC STORE

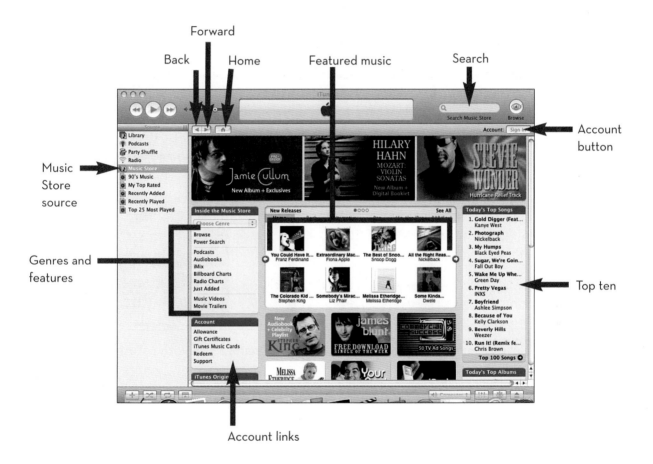

Forward

Back Home Featured music Search

Music Store source

Genres and features

Account button

Top ten

Account links

SETTING UP AN ACCOUNT AT THE MUSIC STORE

If you don't already have an account with Apple (you do if you use .Mac or buy products from Apple's online store), you need to set one up before you can buy items from the Music Store. If you do have an account, you'll use your existing username and password to buy music from the store. You do not need an account to browse or preview music.

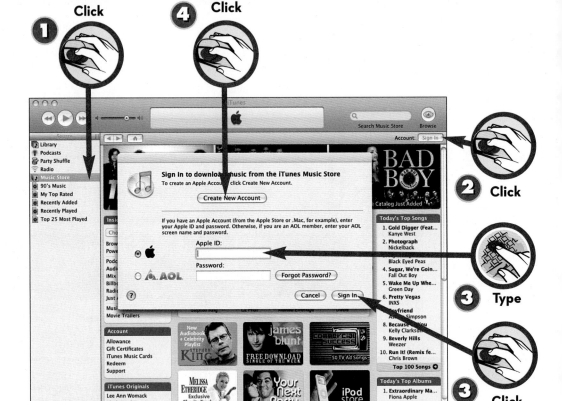

Click ❶

Click ❹

Start

❷ **Click**

❸ **Type**

❸ **Click**

❶ In iTunes, click the **Music Store** item in the source pane to view the store.

❷ Click the **Account** button to enter new or existing account information.

❸ If you have an Apple ID, enter it and your password in the appropriate fields and click **Sign In**.

❹ If you don't have an Apple ID, click **Create New Account**.

Continued

 TIP
Auto Log In
After you have created a Music Store account, the Account button in the upper-right corner of the Music Store window displays your account name instead of Sign In. If you don't see your account name, click **Sign In** and enter your Apple ID and password.

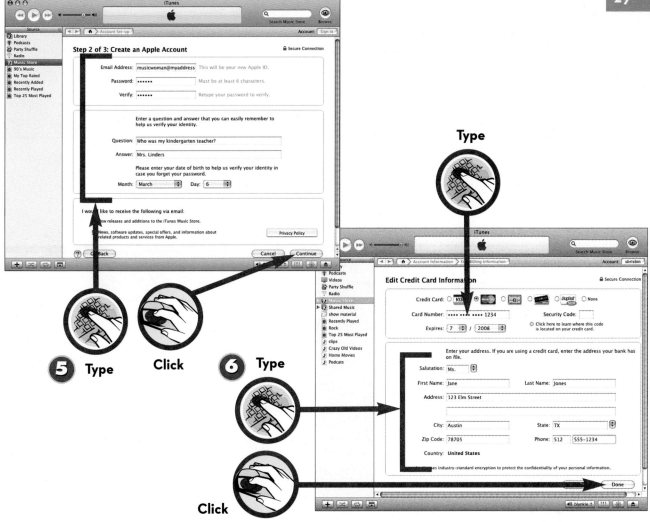

Type

5 **Type**　**Click**　6 **Type**

Click

5 Read the license agreement and click **Continue**. In the Step 2 of 3 account creation screen, enter the email address you want to use as your new Apple ID. You also enter a password and a security question. Click **Continue**.

6 Enter credit card information on the Step 3 of 3 screen. Your card will be charged automatically when you complete a Music Store purchase. Clicking **Done** completes the process and logs you into your new Music Store account.

End

TIP
Buy with Your AOL Account
You can use your AOL account to buy music. When you click the Account button to sign in, click the **AOL** button and then enter your AOL screen name and password. Your purchases will appear on your next AOL bill.

TIP
Changing Account Options
If you need to update information about your account, click the **Account** button (it displays your Apple ID or email address), enter your password, and then click **Edit Account Information**.

SETTING SHOPPING PREFERENCES

After you have an account, you need to choose how your purchase requests will be handled. You can choose to add items to a shopping cart and check out when you're done shopping, or use the 1-Click feature to buy items immediately.

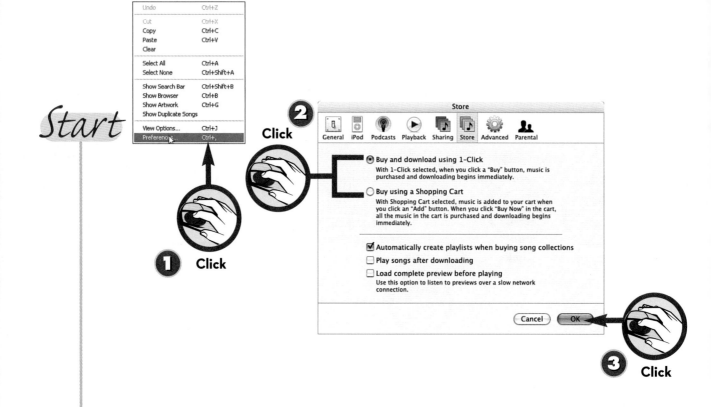

Start

Click

Click

1 **Click**

3 **Click**

1 While logged into your Music Store account, choose **iTunes**, **Preferences** for Mac or **Edit**, **Preferences** for Windows, and then click the **Store** tab.

2 Choose either **Buy and Download Using 1-Click** or **Buy Using a Shopping Cart**. The 1-Click option sends your purchase request immediately when you click Buy Song or Buy Album in the Music Store without giving you the option of reviewing the order. A shopping cart holds all items you want to buy until you check out and empty your cart.

3 Click **OK** to close the Preferences dialog.

End

NOTE

A 1-Click Wonder

Using the Music Store's 1-Click option is the quickest way to buy music, and eliminates the clicks required to work with a shopping cart. On the other hand, using a shopping cart allows you to consolidate purchases into a single transaction on your credit card statement. It's also easier to keep track of how much money you're spending on music.

SEARCHING THE MUSIC STORE

You can use iTunes's powerful search feature to search for items by artist, song name, album name, genre, and item type (music, podcasts, and audiobooks).

Type ①

Start

② **Click**

③ **Click**

④ **Click**

① Type **apple** in the iTunes search field on any Music Store page and press **Return** or **Enter**. The Music Store returns all results for artists, songs, and albums with *apple* in their names.

② Click the **Music** and **Name** buttons on the search bar to limit search results to songs with *apple* in their titles. The window changes to show only songs that match your search.

③ Click **Artist** to find performers and bands with *apple* in their names.

④ If you see an artist you're interested in, click the name or a specific album.

End

NOTE

New Search

At any point in your search of the Music Store, entering new text in the search field starts a brand-new search.

BROWSING THE MUSIC STORE

The Music Store works very much like a web browser. Click on links or images to view sub-categories or individual items. Use the Back, Forward, and Home keys to move between windows.

Start

1. On the Music Store home page, click the image for one of the featured albums.

2. You'll see an enlarged version of the album art, plus details about the album and related links. Scroll the window to read reviews of this album.

3. To view more music by this artist, click the artist's name in the upper portion of the window.

4. Click the **Back** button to return to the previous page.

Continued

TIP

See an Artist Page

To read more about an artist, to get links to other albums and iTunes areas featuring the artist, and to get links to the band's website, click one of the small buttons to the right of the artist's name in the lower portion of the window.

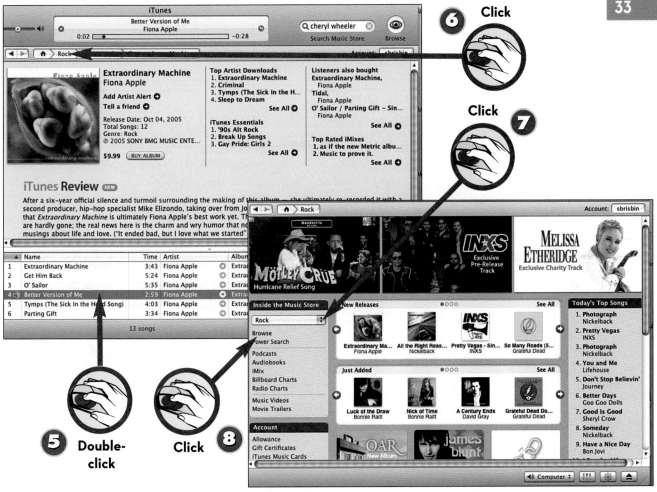

5 In the lower pane, double-click a song from the album to hear a preview.

6 Click the genre button to view a page featuring more artists in this category.

7 On the Music Store home page, choose another genre from the drop-down list below the **Inside the Music Store** heading.

8 Click **Browse** to see a folder-like listing of Music Store contents.

End

TIP

Browse Back and Forth

You can retrace your steps in the Music Store just as you can on a website. Use the Back and Forward arrows above the Music Store browser to return to pages you've visited before. The label to the right of the Home button enables you to move to genre and artist pages.

BUYING A SONG FROM THE MUSIC STORE

The beauty of the Music Store is that almost all individual songs cost the same—$.99. If you find one you like, buy it using your Apple or AOL account, and it is downloaded to your computer.

Start

Click **2**

Click **1**

1 In the Music Store's lower pane, find a song you want to buy. Click the **Buy Song** button to the right of the price. (If you don't see the Buy Song button, expand the iTunes window to the right.)

2 If you've chosen 1-Click shopping, you'll see a dialog box asking if you are sure you want to buy the song. Click **Buy** to confirm. iTunes downloads your new song.

Continued

NOTE

Buy in One Shot

Songs you add to your Music Store shopping cart remain in the cart until you buy them, even if you quit iTunes. A shopping cart is a great way to hold a group of songs until you're ready to buy them all.

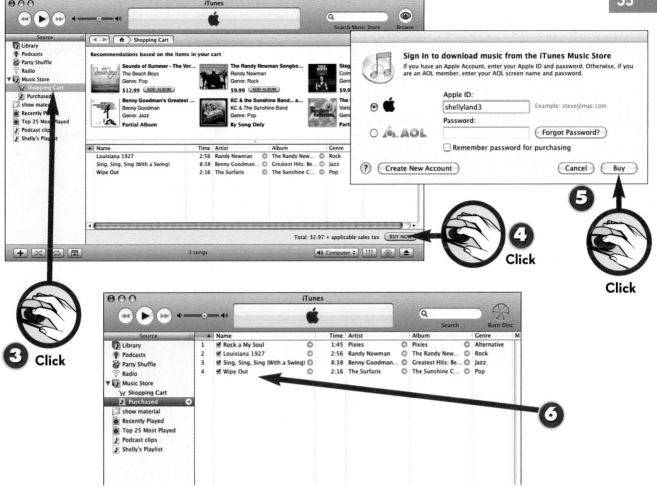

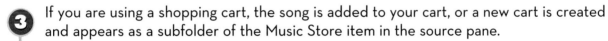

3 If you are using a shopping cart, the song is added to your cart, or a new cart is created and appears as a subfolder of the Music Store item in the source pane.

4 When you're ready to buy the items in your shopping cart, select the cart and click the **Buy Now** button at the bottom of the shopping cart window.

5 iTunes asks you to verify your password. Click **Buy**, and then **Buy** again when asked if you're sure. Your songs are downloaded.

6 Music Store downloads appear in the **Purchased** playlist in the source pane. They're also added to your iTunes library.

End

NOTE

Keep Track of Purchases

The Purchased playlist contains all files you've downloaded from the Music Store using this computer. Downloaded songs are also available in the iTunes library. You can add a purchased song to any iTunes playlist by dragging it onto the playlist's name in the source pane.

BUYING AN ALBUM FROM THE MUSIC STORE

Although some artists and record companies offer only individual songs on the Music Store, most music is available for purchase in album form. If you want a complete album, you can usually save a few dollars over the cost of the individual songs.

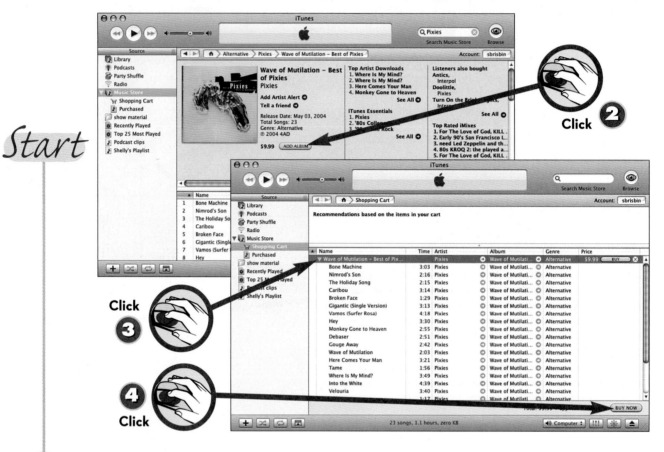

Start

Click **3**

4 Click

1 Find an album you want to purchase. View the album's page by clicking its album art.

2 Click the **Add Album** (or **Buy Album** if you use 1-Click) button.

3 The album is downloaded or added to your shopping cart. If you use the shopping cart, click the disclosure triangle to see individual songs.

4 Click **Buy Now**, and then **Buy** in the dialog that appears, to complete the transaction.

End

TIP
Do Over
If you've changed your mind about an item in the shopping cart before the purchase is complete, you can remove it from the shopping cart by clicking the **X** to the right of the Buy button.

USING POWER SEARCH

If you know what you want but can't seem to find it, try Power Search, which enables you to use multiple criteria to find items you're looking for in the Music Store.

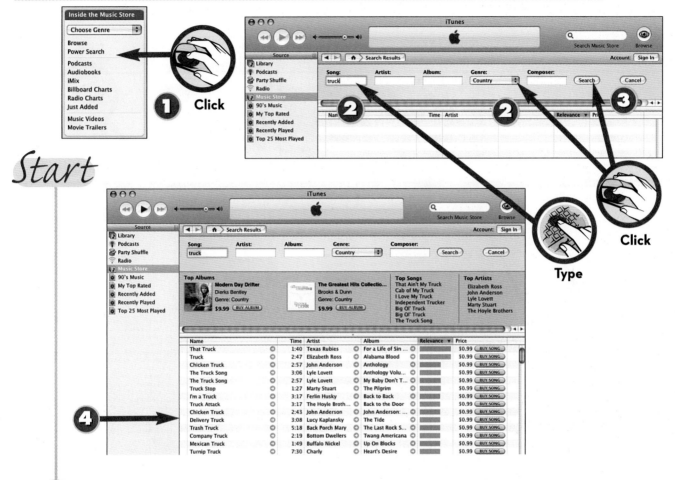

Start

1 Click the **Power Search** link on the Inside the Music Store navigation pane.

2 Type search terms in one or more fields in the Power Search window to search for items. Try *truck* in the **Song** field, and then choose **Country** from the genre menu.

3 Click **Search**.

4 Results containing all of the search terms appear. From here you can preview or buy songs.

End

TIP

Power Search Across Mediums

Because Power Search includes buttons for all of the types of media in the Music Store, you might begin a search for music and quickly progress to finding related audiobooks, podcasts, and videos.

BROWSING CHARTS

The Music Store organizes music in many ways. Besides the genres listed in the Inside the Music Store navigation pane, you can also browse through radio airplay listings and previous years' *Billboard* magazine charts.

Start

Click

Click ②

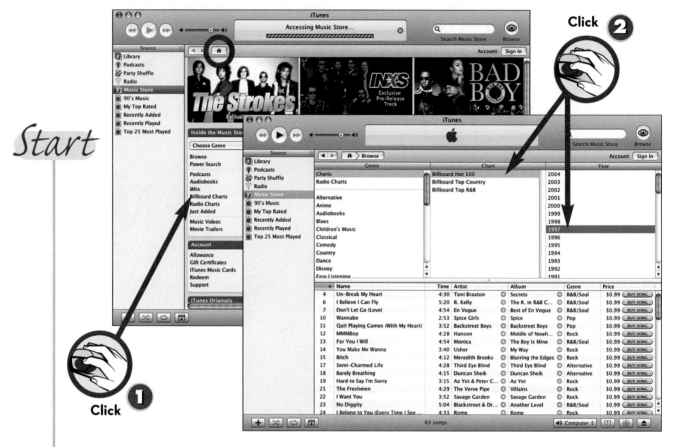

1. From the home page of the Music Store (click the Home button if you need to get there), click **Billboard Charts**.

2. In the browser window, click **Billboard Hot 100** in the Chart column and choose a year. That year's top songs appear in the pane below. From here you can preview or buy them.

End

TIP
Radio City
To see a chart for a radio station you like, click **Radio Charts**, and then a city and the station.

NOTE
More Browsing
As you probably noticed when you browsed for charts, the Music Store's genres are also available from the browser. In many cases, genres have subgenres that appear in the middle pane when you click a top-level genre.

CHECKING OUT iMIXES

An iMix is a group of songs compiled by a Music Store customer. iMixes appear on individual artists' pages, or you can browse them from the Music Store home page.

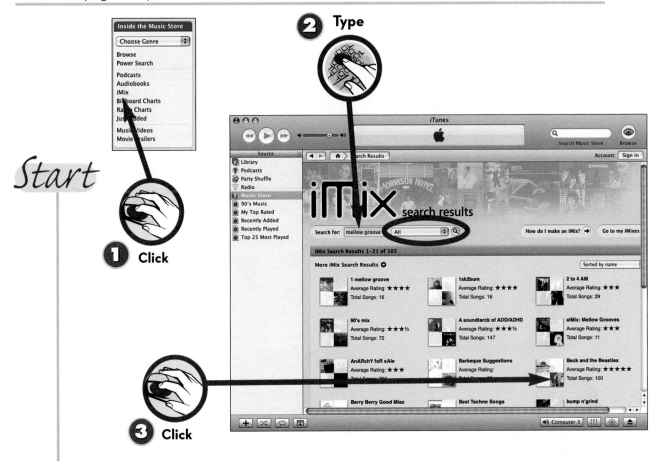

Type 2

Start

1 Click

3 Click

1 On the Music Store home page, click **iMix** in the Inside the Music Store navigation pane.

2 Type **mellow groove** into the iMix search field. Leave **All** selected on the menu. You can also search by artist, album, or song name.

3 Click a highly rated iMix to see and preview its songs. You can buy any or all songs in the mix if you want.

End

BUYING AUDIOBOOKS

Like music, audiobooks are available for purchase and download from the Music Store. You can use the same search and browsing tools to locate them, or begin in the Audiobooks section of the Music Store.

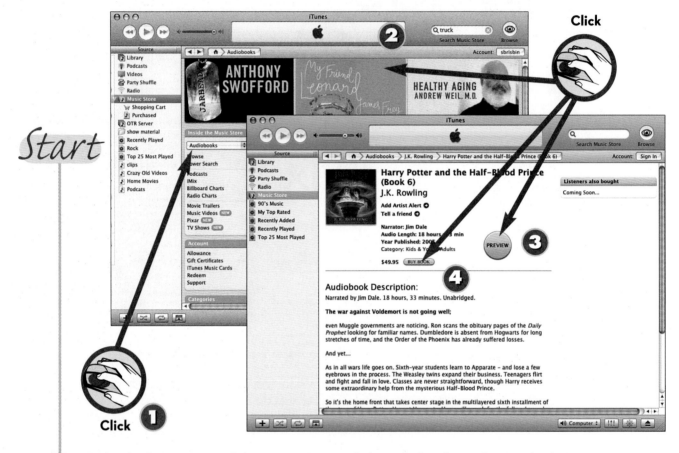

Start

Click **1**

Click

End

1 From the home page of the Music Store, click **Audiobooks** in the Inside the Music Store navigation pane. The featured content changes from music to books.

2 Click a featured or top-ranked book to see details.

3 To hear a sample of the book, click **Preview**.

4 Click **Buy Book** (if using 1-Click) or **Add Book** (if using the shopping cart) to make a purchase.

TIP

Categories
To browse audiobooks by type, scroll down to the **Categories** section of the navigation pane and click one.

ALLOWANCES AND GIFT CERTIFICATES

If there's a music lover in your life, you can make a gift of items from the Music Store either by sending a one-time gift certificate or by creating a regular music allowance that allows your lucky family member or friend to buy a preset amount of music each month.

Scroll

Start

Click ①

② **Type**

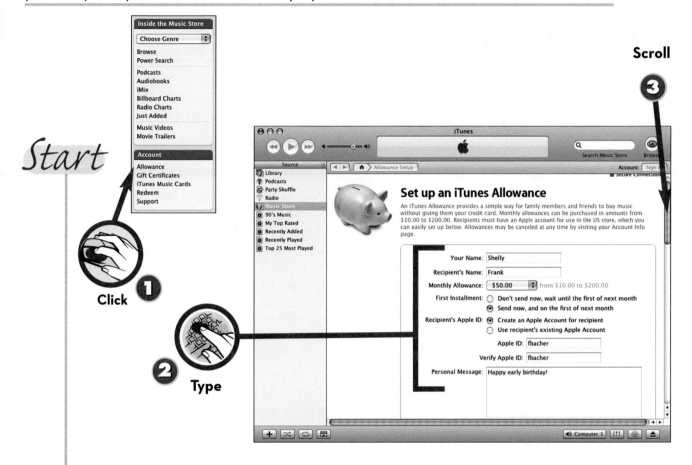

Inside the Music Store

Choose Genre

Browse
Power Search

Podcasts
Audiobooks
iMix
Billboard Charts
Radio Charts
Just Added

Music Videos
Movie Trailers

Account

Allowance
Gift Certificates
iTunes Music Cards
Redeem
Support

Set up an iTunes Allowance

An iTunes Allowance provides a simple way for family members and friends to buy music without giving them your credit card. Monthly allowances can be purchased in amounts from $10.00 to $200.00. Recipients must have an Apple account for use in the US store, which you can easily set up below. Allowances may be canceled at any time by visiting your Account Info page.

Your Name:	Shelly
Recipient's Name:	Frank
Monthly Allowance:	$50.00 — from $10.00 to $200.00
First Installment:	○ Don't send now, wait until the first of next month
	● Send now, and on the first of next month
Recipient's Apple ID:	● Create an Apple Account for recipient
	○ Use recipient's existing Apple Account
Apple ID:	fbacher
Verify Apple ID:	fbacher
Personal Message:	Happy early birthday!

① On the Music Store home page, click **Allowance** in the Account navigation pane.

② Enter your name, your recipient's name, and the amount of the music allowance you want to give. Enter either your recipient's current Apple ID or create one for them. The ID is needed to use the allowance account. You can also enter a personal message.

③ Be sure to scroll down and read the Terms and Conditions below the form, and then press **Return** or **Enter** to continue.

④ If you are creating a new Apple ID, be sure to tell your recipient his or her new ID and password.

End

NOTE
Allowance Alternatives
An allowance is basically a gift certificate you can give each month. The Music Store also offers one-time gift certificates under the Gift Certificate link on the home page. Redeem gift certificates you have been given from this link.

NOTE
Password Setting
After you have entered the allowance information, you are asked to enter a password for your recipient. This password, along with the Apple ID you entered for the recipient, is needed to access the recipient's allowance.

ALL ABOUT iTUNES PLAYLISTS

As you've already learned, the music library contains links to all of the files you have imported or downloaded to your computer using iTunes. You have probably also noticed the other items in the iTunes source pane: Podcasts, Videos, Party Shuffle, Radio, 90's Music, My Top Rated, Recently Added, Recently Played, and Top 25 Most Played. These items are called *playlists*, and you use them to organize your audio files. You also use playlists to tell iTunes which songs and other files to add to your iPod when you synchronize it with your computer. Two of the playlists (Radio and Party Shuffle) have special features that are described throughout this part. You'll learn about the Podcast playlist in Part 8, "Finding and Listening to Podcasts," and the Videos playlist in Part 9, "Watching Video in iTunes and on Your iPod."

In addition to using the playlists provided for you, you can create your own, organizing your music by genre, artist, or in any other way that matches how you listen. You can also create folders to keep your playlists organized. *Smart playlists* use rules that build a playlist for you. Tell iTunes, for example, to put all songs purchased in the past month into a New Stuff playlist, or make one that automatically gathers all of your reggae and ska tunes. Smart playlists are updated automatically when matching items are added to your library.

You can include a song, audiobook, or podcast in as many playlists as you like. A playlist is simply a group of pointers, so creating one does not move files around or change your iTunes library.

Finally, you can use playlists to tell iTunes to sync selected items to your iPod. You'll learn more in Part 6, "Setting Up Your iPod," about how all this works.

iTUNES PLAYLISTS

Special
playlists

Shared music

Playlist folder

Included
smart playlists

Standard
playlist

Smart playlist

CREATING A PLAYLIST

Standard playlists contain whatever items you add to them. You might create a playlist for favorite artists, a group of tunes you like to hear together, or a favorite type of music.

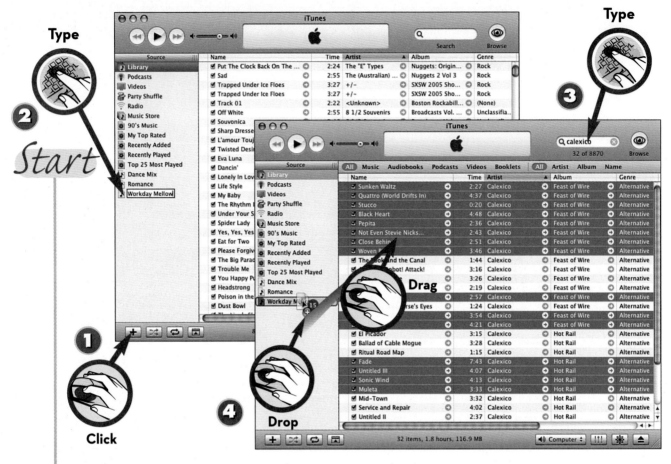

1. In iTunes, click the **Create a Playlist** button. An untitled playlist appears, with its name selected.

2. Type a name for your new playlist.

3. Type the name of a favorite artist in the **Search** field. All songs by that artist appear in the content pane.

4. Select all of the songs you want to add to the new playlist, and drag the group onto the playlist's name.

TIP

Express Playlist Creation

To quickly create a playlist, find or browse to the songs you want to include and select them. Choose **File**, **New Playlist from Selection**. You can type a new name for the new playlist.

TIP

Natural Selection

To select all items that are visible in the iTunes content pane, press **Ctrl+A** (Windows) or ⌘**+A** (Mac). To select some but not all items, click the first item and then **Ctrl+click** (Windows) or ⌘**+click** (Mac) additional items.

ADDING AND DELETING SONGS FROM PLAYLISTS

You can add or remove items in a standard playlist at any time.

Start

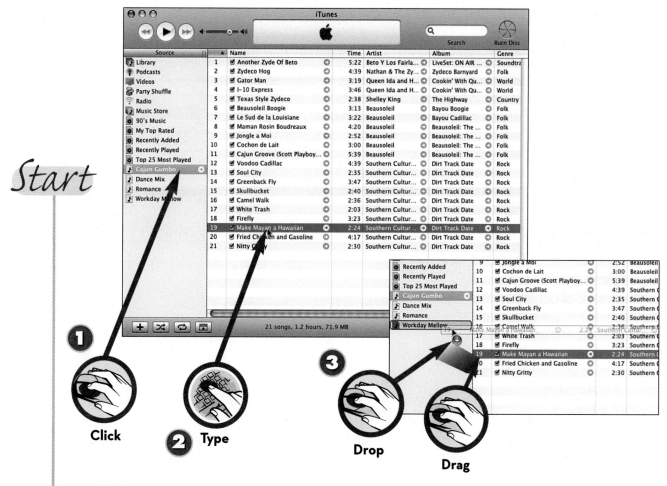

① **Click**

② **Type**

③ **Drop**

Drag

① In the **source** pane, click a playlist you have created.

② To delete a song from the playlist, select it and press **Delete**. The file is removed from the playlist, but not from the library.

③ To add a song to a different playlist, select the song and drag it onto the other playlist. The song is copied to the second playlist and remains in the first.

End

 TIP

Remove, Don't Delete

When you remove an item from a playlist by pressing the **Delete** key, the item leaves the playlist, but is not removed from your music library. To remove an item from the playlist and the iTunes library, press **Shift+Delete** (Windows) or **Option+Delete** (Mac).

 TIP

Skip, Don't Remove

If you want to skip a song while playing a playlist but don't want to remove the song, uncheck the check box next to the song you don't want to hear. iTunes skips unchecked songs.

USING SMART PLAYLISTS

A *smart playlist* consists of songs that have at least one thing in common: an artist, a genre, or other descriptive element listed in their ID3 tags. You can choose more than one element, or create a playlist that includes a certain type of song and excludes certain items within that group (Led Zeppelin songs that don't have *heaven* in the title, for example). To get an idea of what smart playlists can do, begin with those included with iTunes.

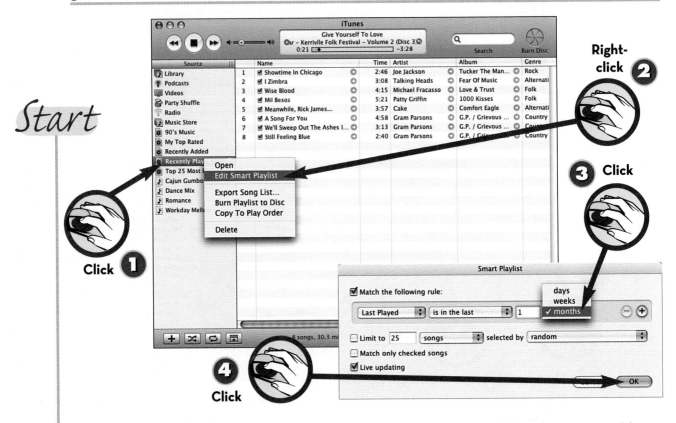

1. Click the **Recently Played Playlist** in the source pane. It contains just what you would expect—songs you have played. iTunes added each after it was played.

2. **Right-click** (Windows) or **Control+click** (Mac) on the Recently Played playlist, and choose **Edit Smart Playlist** from the menu.

3. Click the drop-down menu and change Weeks to **Months**. Change 2 to **1** in the adjacent field. The Recently Played playlist now displays songs played in the previous month.

4. Click **OK** to close the Smart Playlist dialog box, and notice that more songs appear on the playlist.

End

— NOTE

More Included Smart Playlists
Top 25 Most Played, Recently Added, and 90's Music are also built-in iTunes playlists. Like Recently Played, Top 25 Most Played and Recently Added get their information from iTunes itself. 90's Music, on the other hand, uses the tags associated with a song. A song with a year tag between 1990 and 1999 is added to the playlist.

USING PLAYLIST FOLDERS

Like a folder on your computer, an iTunes folder stores multiple items. You can create a folder to group playlists that are similar in content. Folders can hold both standard and smart playlists.

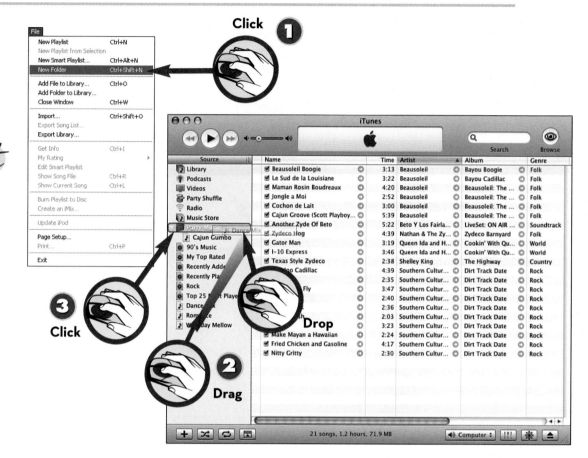

Start

Click ①

Click ③

Drag ②

Drop

① In iTunes, choose **File**, **New Folder**. While the folder is selected, type a name for it.

② Drag a playlist onto the folder. You can select multiple playlists by ⌘**+clicking** (Mac) or **Ctrl+clicking** (Windows) them, and then dragging them onto the folder.

③ Click the folder's expansion triangle to see and use the playlists you added.

End

CREATING A SMART PLAYLIST

Creating a smart playlist with rules that tell iTunes which tracks to include allows you to keep your library organized, even when you add new music. That's because iTunes adds any item that matches the criteria you've set to the smart playlist. Like a standard playlist, you can sync smart playlists with your iPod.

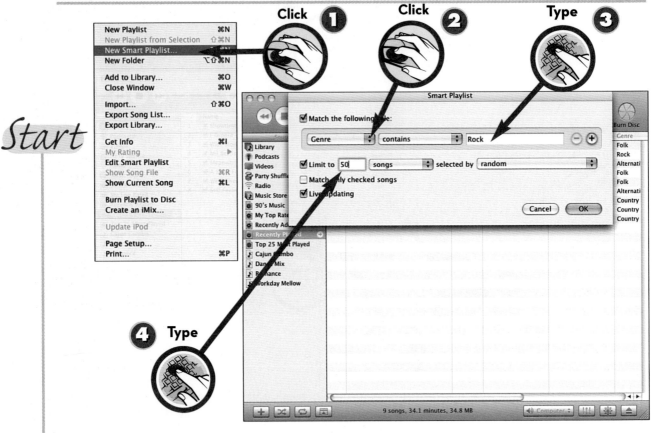

Start

Click ➊ **Click** ➋ **Type** ➌

➍ **Type**

➊ Choose **File, New Smart Playlist**.

➋ In the dialog box that appears, choose **Genre** from the drop-down menu.

➌ Type **Rock** in the field on the right to include all songs in a genre whose name includes rock. As you type, iTunes begins to fill in the genre, based on your library.

➍ Click the **Limit To** check box and type **50**, to limit the smart playlist's size. If the box is left unchecked, all of the matching songs are included.

Continued

TIP

Any or All

If you set multiple rules for a smart playlist, iTunes finds only those items that match all of the rules you've created. Choose **Any** from the menu at the top of the **Edit Smart Playlist** dialog if you want to find songs that match any of the criteria.

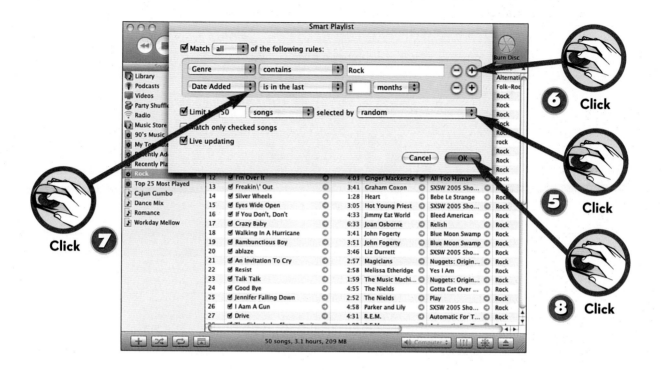

5 Use the **Selected By** menu if you want to give preference to items from a particular artist, play count, or other criteria.

6 Click the **Add Rule** button (+ sign) to the right of the field to reveal a second line where you can type a criteria for the playlist.

7 Choose **Date Added** from the first drop-down menu and **Is in the Last** from the middle menu. Choose **Months** from the final menu to find songs added less than one month ago.

8 Click **OK** to complete the playlist.

End

-TIP-
Smart Squared
Did you know that a smart playlist can use another playlist (even a smart one) as a criterion? For example, let's say you have playlists for several favorite artists, but would like to hear them all together. You could create a new smart playlist using each artist's name as a criterion, but the easier way is to select **Playlist** from the left drop-down menu in the Smart Playlist dialog, and then the name of a playlist from the right menu. Repeat this for each playlist you want to add to your new smart playlist.

USING THE PARTY SHUFFLE PLAYLIST

Party Shuffle is a special iTunes playlist that creates a list of the songs that will be played next in iTunes. You can use Party Shuffle to play a random group of songs from the library or a playlist, or you can rearrange the list of upcoming songs to suit your mood.

Start

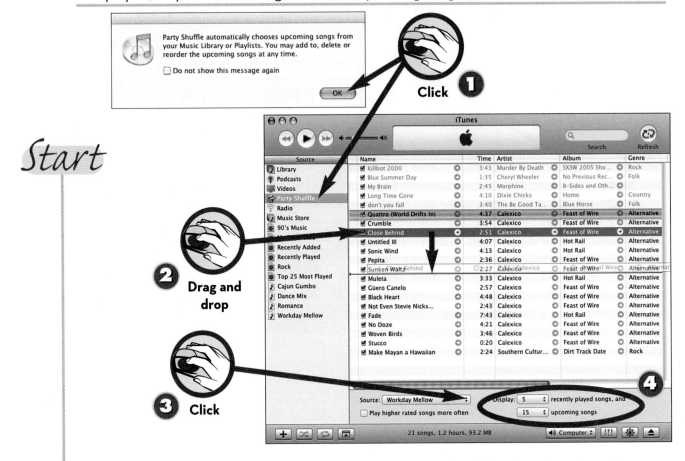

1. Click **Party Shuffle** in the source pane, and click **OK** in the dialog box describing Party Shuffle.
2. Drag the first song downward to change the play order. Select a song you don't want to hear, and press **Delete**. The song is deleted from the Party Shuffle, not your library.
3. Choose a playlist from the **Source** drop-down menu to shuffle that playlist. You can move or remove items.
4. From the **Display** menus, choose how many recently played and upcoming songs you want to include.

End

NOTE

Quick Shuffle

Party Shuffle works at any time. You can change the play order before you begin playing or after the playlist has started.

USING THE RADIO PLAYLIST

Unlike other playlists, Radio features links to content, even before you fill your iTunes library with songs and other items. Organized into categories, Radio contains links to Internet radio stations that stream their content on the Internet. You need to be connected to the Internet to use the Radio playlist, and a high-speed connection is highly recommended.

1 Click

Start

2 Click

3 Double-click

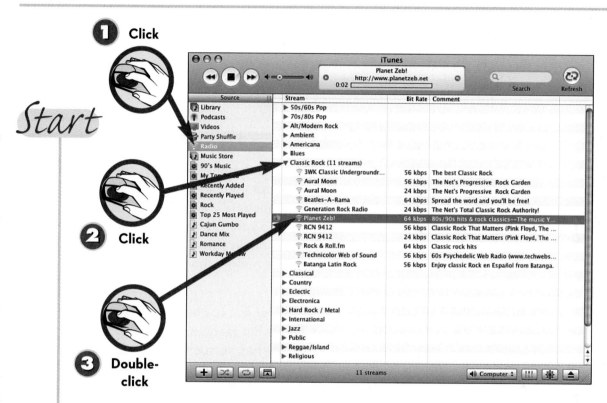

1 Click **Radio** in the source pane.

2 Expand the Classic Rock genre by clicking on the triangle to the left of its name.

3 Double-click an item to hear the radio station. It might take a few seconds to connect.

End

TIP

Save Your Station

If you really like a certain radio station, you can save a link to it in your iTunes library or in a playlist. Just select the station you like and drag it onto the library or onto a playlist.

NOTE

Radio Tuner

If you're really into streaming radio, create a playlist just for your favorite radio stations. Then drag all of your favorite stations into the playlist.

SETTING UP YOUR iPOD

In this part, we shift from the iTunes library back to your iPod. This part discusses adding songs to the iPod and setting the device up to work the way you want it to.

You can add songs and other items to your iPod in two basic ways: sync the iPod to your iTunes library or copy items to the iPod manually, using drag and drop. The process of syncing means iTunes automatically copies the content of your iTunes music library to your iPod without you having to manually copy anything. The advantage of syncing is that anytime you update your iTunes music library, new items become available to your iPod the next time you connect it. Some people update their iPods manually because their music library is larger than the capacity of their iPod. The middle road for iPod syncing is to sync individual playlists to your iPod.

Options on iPod and iPod nano models allow you to choose preferences for language, date and time, display, and even what menu items appear on the device's screen. The screenless iPod shuffle has no such options, but there are still a few sync settings you can configure for the shuffle in iTunes. Look for tasks within this part that are specific to the shuffle because the instructions differ from syncing and configuring the other iPod models.

iPOD SYNCING

iTunes info display

iPod source

iPod podcasts playlist

iPod music playlist

iPod shuffle source

iPod shuffle options

SYNCING AN iPod FOR THE FIRST TIME

After you have installed iPod software, as described in Part 2, "Connecting Your iPod to a Mac or PC," and added music to iTunes as described in subsequent parts, you can add music to the iPod by syncing it to your computer. Your first sync creates a playlist in iTunes and an identical one on the iPod. You can sync the entire contents of your music library (or a random selection of songs, if your iPod can't hold it all).

Start

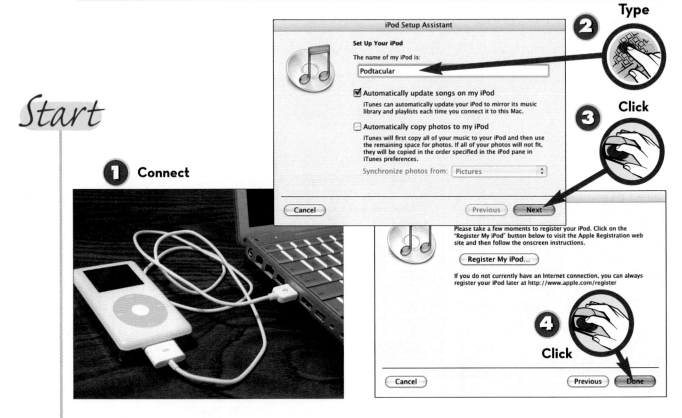

1 Connect

Type

2

Click

3

4

Click

---

1 Connect an iPod to your computer.

2 In the dialog box that appears, type a name for the iPod and be sure that the **Automatically Update Songs on My iPod** check box is checked.

3 Click **Next**.

4 Click **Done**. If you've already registered your iPod, as described in Part 2, there's no need to register it again.

Continued

TIP
Playlists for Later
Even if your music library does fit on your iPod and you decide to sync the entire library when you first connect the device, you can change your syncing options later to use specific playlists, as described later in this part.

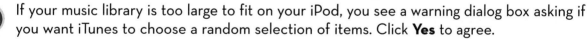

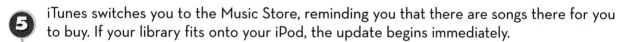

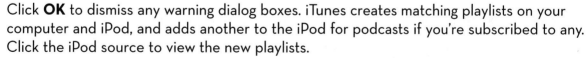

5 iTunes switches you to the Music Store, reminding you that there are songs there for you to buy. If your library fits onto your iPod, the update begins immediately.

6 If your music library is too large to fit on your iPod, you see a warning dialog box asking if you want iTunes to choose a random selection of items. Click **Yes** to agree.

7 Click **OK** to dismiss any warning dialog boxes. iTunes creates matching playlists on your computer and iPod, and adds another to the iPod for podcasts if you're subscribed to any. Click the iPod source to view the new playlists.

End

🚀 **TIP**

But I Don't Like Those Songs!

If iTunes is forced to choose a selection of songs to add to your iPod because your music library is larger than the iPod's capacity, you might end up with music you don't really want, or find that a favorite song is missing. You will be able to make changes to the iPod's contents by adding and removing items from the iPod selection playlist in iTunes, and then syncing the playlist to your iPod, as described later in this part.

MANAGING AN iPOD MANUALLY

Both automatic iPod management methods synchronize your music library and iPod. Managing your iPod manually means you must add and delete each item from the iPod yourself. You can manage the iPod manually from the start, or switch from automatic to manual management later.

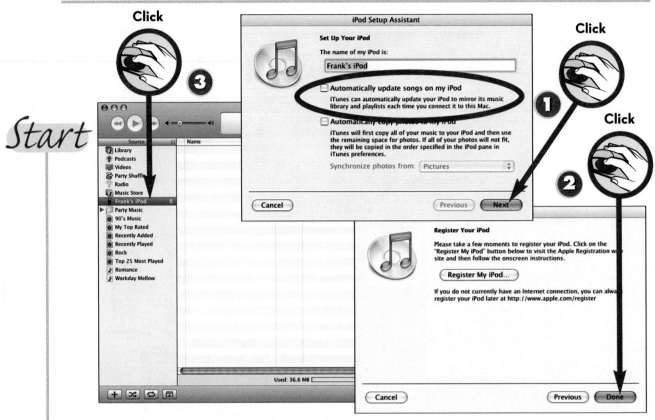

Click   **③**

Start

Click   **①**

Click   **②**

① When connecting the iPod for initial setup, uncheck the **Automatically Update Songs on My iPod** check box and click **Next**.

② Click **Done** in the Register dialog box.

③ iTunes displays the Music Store. Click the **iPod** item in the source pane.

Continued

-TIP-

More Playlists

When you manage the iPod manually, you can create and modify its playlists just as you would an iTunes playlist, adding and deleting them at will, and moving songs from one to another. Like all other iPod playlists, copying is one-way; you can't move music from the iPod to the computer using iTunes.

Click 5

Drag and drop 4

4 Choose an iTunes playlist whose contents you want to add to your iPod and drag the playlist onto the iPod item. The playlist's contents are copied to your iPod. Drag more songs into the iPod playlist, whether you dragged the playlist from your music library, or created it from scratch.

5 With the iPod selected, choose **File, New Smart Playlist**. Choose options for the smart playlist. The smart playlist is built from the contents of your iPod, not your iTunes music library.

End

TIP

Another Plus

Another way to manually add tunes to your iPod is to, with the iPod item selected, click the ✦ button (below the source pane), and type a name for the new playlist that then appears under the iPod item.

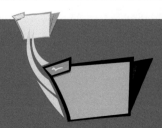

ADDING PLAYLISTS TO AN iPOD

After you have synced an iPod to your music library for the first time, you can add more playlists to the sync, or change the playlists that are already synced. This is also a great way to organize the music you want to add to the iPod, even if your music library is too large. You can create new playlists in iTunes or use existing ones.

Start

Click

1 In iTunes, create playlists that you want to sync with your iPod, or choose from the existing playlists. Choose **iTunes**, **Preferences** (Mac) or **Edit**, **Prefrences** (Windows).

2 Click **iPod**.

3 Click the **Automatically Update Selected Playlists Only** radio button.

4 Choose playlists to add to your iPod by clicking their check boxes. Click **OK**.

End

NOTE

No Dupes, Please

Like iTunes playlists, iPod playlists are simply pointers to songs. Including a single song in multiple playlists does not result in multiple copies of the song on your iPod.

TIP

Organizing for the Pod

One way to keep iPod playlists organized is to put them all in a single folder in iTunes. Create your iPod playlists, and then add them to a new folder named for your iPod. You will still need to add the individual playlists in iTunes Preferences as shown in this task.

SYNCING AN iPOD

After you have linked an iTunes playlist with your iPod, iTunes syncs it with your music library whenever you connect the iPod. You can also manually sync at any time while the iPod is connected. For instructions on syncing a shuffle, see the next task, "Adding Music to an iPod Shuffle."

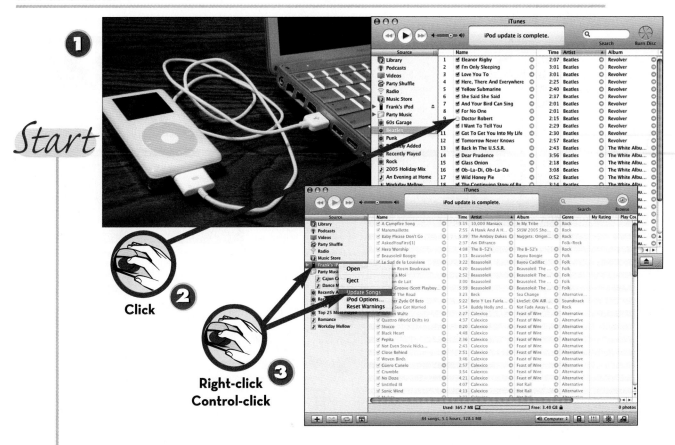

Start

Click

2

3

**Right-click
Control-click**

1 Connect your iPod to the computer. Automatic synchronization begins, unless you are managing the iPod manually (see "Managing an iPod Manually" earlier in this part for more on manual updating).

2 Make a change to a playlist that is synced with your iPod; add or delete a song, for example.

3 Right-click (Windows) or Control-click (Mac) the **iPod** in the source pane and choose **Update Songs**. iTunes synchronizes your iPod with your music library or playlists.

End

TIP

Remove, Don't Delete
When you remove an item from a playlist by pressing the **Delete** key, the item leaves the playlist, but is not removed from your music library. To remove an item from the playlist and the iTunes library, press **Shift+Delete** (Windows) or **Option+Delete** (Mac).

ADDING MUSIC TO AN iPOD SHUFFLE

The procedure for adding songs to an iPod shuffle is similar, but not identical, to that used by other iPods. You can add songs automatically, point the shuffle to a specific playlist in iTunes, or manage the shuffle manually. Unlike other iPods, the iPod shuffle does not have its own playlists. Also unlike other iPods, the shuffle allows you to use multiple syncing options together.

Start

① Plug the iPod shuffle into your computer's **USB port**. If the shuffle is configured to add songs automatically, iTunes copies a random selection.

② Select the iPod **shuffle** in the iTunes source pane.

③ Choose a specific playlist, or leave **Library** selected to tell iTunes where to get songs to add to the shuffle.

④ Click **Choose Songs Randomly** to randomly copy songs, and **Choose Higher Rated Songs More Often** to give a boost to songs you've given four or five stars.

Continued

TIP

Keep Your Shuffle Mounted

To keep the iPod shuffle item in the source pane, even when the device is not connected to your computer, click the **Options** button in iTunes, and click the **Keep This iPod in the Source List** check box. This option allows you to change shuffle options, and add or delete items. Your changes will be applied to the shuffle the next time you connect it to the computer.

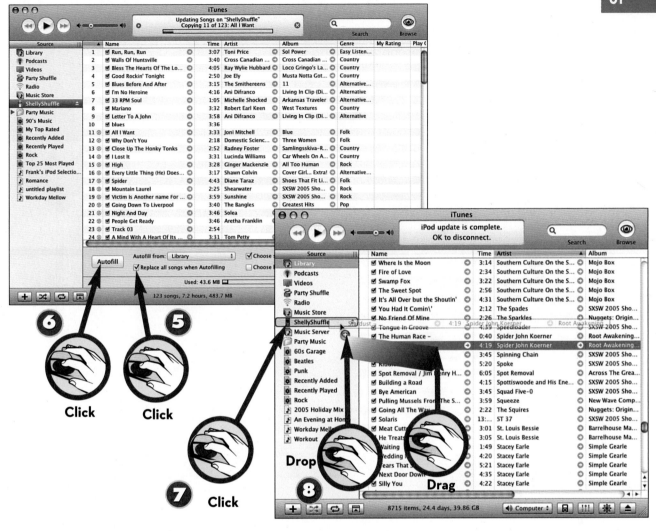

Click   **Click**

Drop

Click

Drag

5️⃣ Clicking the **Replace All Songs When Autofilling** box empties the iPod before adding new songs.

6️⃣ Click the **AutoFill** button to add a random selection of songs to the shuffle. After the update, you can disconnect the iPod shuffle from your computer or make further changes.

7️⃣ To delete an item from the shuffle, first select the **Shuffle** item in the source pane, and then the item. Press **Delete**.

8️⃣ To add an item, drag it from the iTunes **library** onto the Shuffle item.

End

TIP

Switch Playlists Anytime

If you're a shuffle user who likes to change your mind a lot, the shuffle can deal. Anytime you want to change a link between an iTunes playlist and your iPod shuffle, just select the shuffle, choose a new playlist from the **Autofill** drop-down menu, and click **Autofill** to replace the shuffle's previous contents.

DISCONNECTING AN iPOD

iPod models other than the iPod shuffle require you to unmount them from your computer before you can physically disconnect them.

Updating iPod.
Do not disconnect.

Unsafe to disconnect during sync

1

3 Click

Start

Click **2**

① With an iPod connected and mounted in iTunes, check the iTunes display to be sure that the iPod is not currently being synced.

② Click the **iPod** item in the source pane.

③ Click **Eject**. The iPod item disappears from iTunes.

④ Wait for the iTunes display to indicate that the update is complete or to display the Apple logo, and the iPod display to show menus. Then disconnect the iPod from the computer.

End

SETTING iPOD DISPLAY OPTIONS

When you use your iPod for the first time, you can set a number of options that customize the way its menus look and work. These options aren't available on the iPod shuffle, which does not have a screen.

Start

Press
2

1
Press

1 With your iPod charged and disconnected from the computer, activate it by pressing the **center button**.

2 Choose your preferred language from the list, and use the click wheel to navigate to it (move the wheel clockwise to go down the menus and counterclockwise to go up). Then press the **center button** to choose the language.

End

TIP
Menu Navigations
You'll use three buttons—Play, Menu, and the center button—along with the click wheel to navigate iPod menus. Because iPod menus are hierarchical, you might occasionally get lost. If you do, press the **Menu** button to go up one menu level, and press it again to go further up in the hierarchy.

SETTING DATE AND TIME OPTIONS

After you've set the iPod's clock, you'll see the correct time at the top of the iPod display.

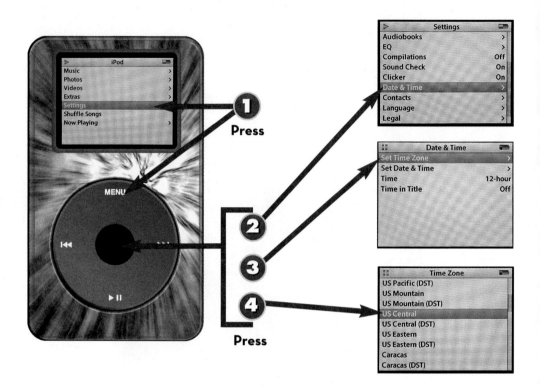

Press

Press

1. Press the **Menu** button to activate the iPod, and choose **Settings** from the menu. If you don't see Settings, press the **Menu** button again to move upward in the hierarchy.

2. Choose **Date & Time**. Use the click wheel to reach it.

3. Select **Set Time Zone**.

4. Choose your time zone from the list. You are then returned to the Date & Time menu.

Continued

─TIP─

Another Way To Deal With Time

Use the iPod's Clock feature to quickly set the iPod's correct time when you travel. You can save clocks for several time zones and choose the one you need when your trip begins. See Part 12, "Using Your iPod As a PDA or Hard Disk."

─ NOTE ─

All Wrapped Up

The iPod skin seen here is available from www.designerskins.com.

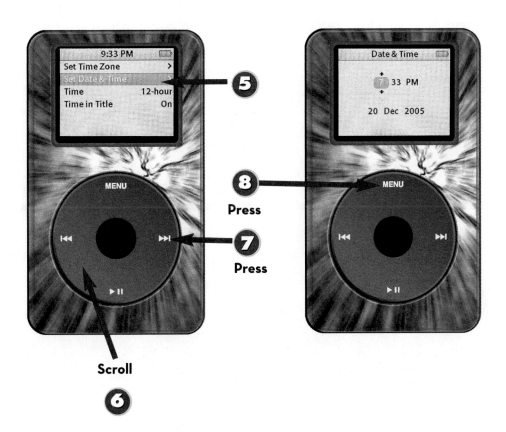

Scroll

5 Choose **Set Date & Time**.

6 If the time is incorrect, use the click wheel to add an hour (scroll clockwise) or go back an hour (scroll counter-clockwise).

7 Press the **Next** button to change minutes, AM/PM, day, month, and/or year.

8 Press **Menu** when you're done to confirm your settings.

 End

TIP
Time in the Title Bar
To see the current time on the iPod's title bar, choose **Time in Title**, and press the **center button** to toggle on the option.

TIP
Backlight Options
To control the iPod's backlight, choose **Backlight Timer** from the **Settings** menu and select the amount of time you want the backlight to remain active from the menu.

CHOOSING iPOD MENUS

By default, the iPod's top-level menu has five items: Music, Photos, Extras, Settings, and Shuffle Songs. The current high-end iPod, sometimes called the video iPod, also has a Videos item. You can add or remove items on the top-level menu, making it easier to find the items you use most often.

Start

1. Choose **Settings** from the top-level menu, and then **Main Menu**.

2. From the list of top-level items and their submenus, select **Playlists**.

3. Press the **center button** to toggle from Off to On.

NOTE

Copied, Not Moved

When you add an item to the main menu, it remains on the submenu where it was before you made the change.

Continued

Press

**Select
and
press**

4 Press the **Menu** button to see your new top-level menu, including Playlists.

5 To remove an item from the top-level menu, go to the Main Menu menu and toggle the item to **Off**.

6 To return the main menu to its original state, choose **Reset Main Menu**, and choose **Reset** when asked to confirm the change.

End

TIP

Menus the Way You Like 'Em

My nominations for best items to add to the main menu are playlists, podcasts, and audiobooks. If you store contacts, calendars, or notes on your iPod, these options should be high on your list for promotion to the main menu.

PLAYING MUSIC

If it feels to you as if we've been getting ready for this chapter for a good many pages, you're right. It's great to know how to set up iTunes and how to load an iPod, but what most people want to do is play some tunes!

iTunes and the iPod share many music playback and browsing features, allowing you to control, navigate, and customize the sound of your tunes.

Like the iPod, and any CD player for that matter, iTunes provides controls for playback, pause, fast forward/rewind, moving between tracks, repeating, and shuffling songs. Those features are roughly duplicated.

iTUNES PLAYBACK CONTROLS

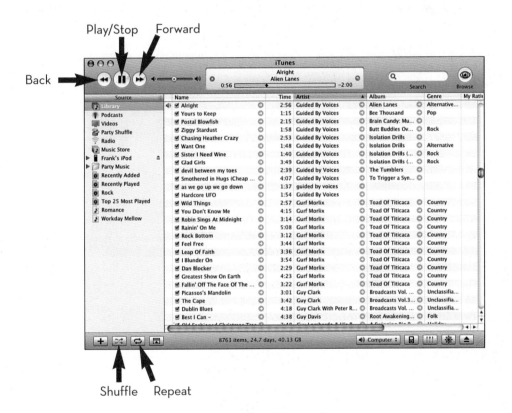

PLAYING A SONG IN iTUNES

You can begin iTunes playback with the click of a button or a push of a key on your keyboard.

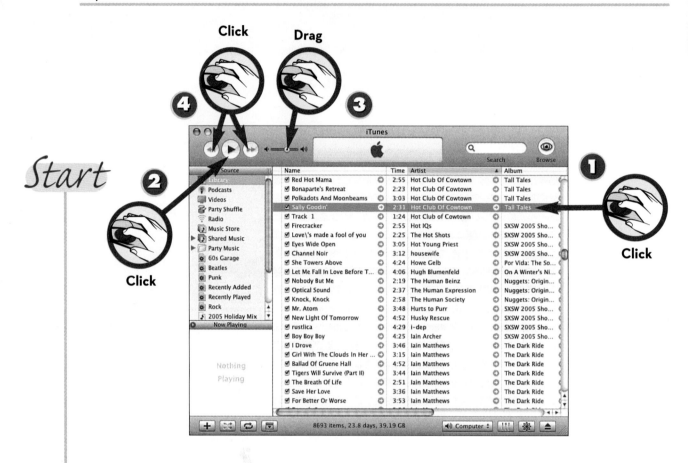

Click **Drag**

Start

Click

Click

1 Click a song in your iTunes music library.

2 Click the **Play** button, or press the spacebar to play the song.

3 Drag the **volume slider** to adjust the sound level.

4 Click the **Forward** button to play the next song or the **Back** button to take you to the previous song.

End

TIP

Double Your Pleasure

You can also play a song by double-clicking it.

TIP

Take the Shortcut

Press ⌘+**right arrow key** (Mac) or **Ctrl+right arrow key** (Windows) to move forward to the next song (or if using the shuffle, to another song). Pressing ⌘+**left arrow** (Mac) or **Ctrl+left arrow** (Windows) takes you to the previous song.

SHUFFLE AND REPEAT

Like a CD player, iTunes can shuffle or repeat your music.

Start

2 Click

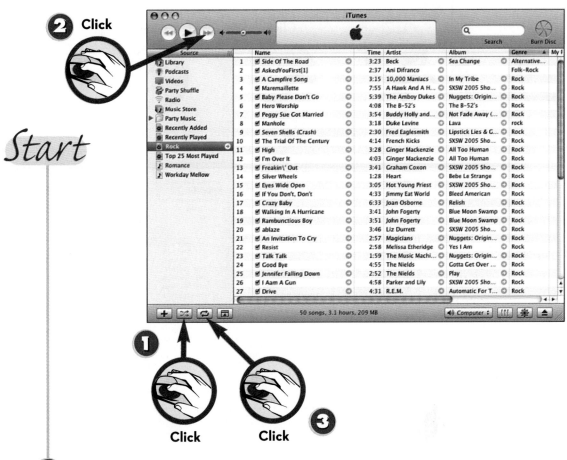

1 Click **Click 3**

 Click the **Shuffle** button.

 Click the **Forward** button. Notice that iTunes jumps to a different song, rather than moving to the next song on the list.

3 Click the **Repeat** button. The current track repeats when it is finished. If you click Repeat again, iTunes repeats the track until you choose another option.

End

— NOTE —

More Than One Way

The Shuffle and Repeat commands also appear on the Controls menu.

—TIP—

Silence

To mute the current track without stopping it, choose **Controls**, **Mute**, or press ⌘**+down arrow** (Mac) or **Ctrl+down arrow** (Windows). To stop playback, click the **Play/Stop** button or press the **spacebar**.

BROWSING IN iTUNES

iTunes's browser feature makes it easier to find music by artist, album, or genre.

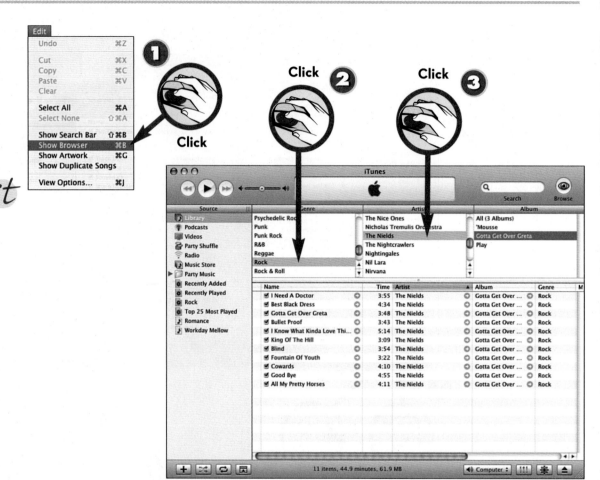

Start

1 Choose **Edit**, **Show Browser**.

2 Select a **genre**. Lists of artists and titles matching the genre you've chosen appear, with individual songs listed below.

3 Click an artist to see albums by that artist, with their songs below.

End

TIP

Browse Playlists

You can use the browser to change your view of the music library or individual playlists. If you switch from the library to a playlist, you'll need to choose **Edit**, **Show Browser** again.

SEARCHING IN iTUNES

The iTunes search field allows you to find items by the contents of their ID3 tags. The search bar enables you to be more precise in your search.

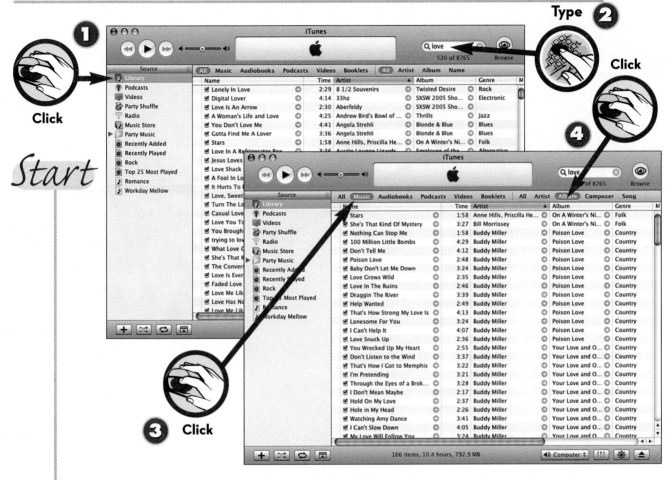

Start

End

1. Click the **Library** item in the iTunes source pane, if it isn't already selected.

2. In the search field, type **love**. Matching items appear in the content pane, with the search bar above. (If you receive no results, type another search term.)

3. Click the **Music** button to narrow your search to songs (excluding audiobooks and podcasts).

4. Click **Album** to see only albums containing the word *love*.

TIP

Browse 'n Search

You can search using the standard iTunes list view, or the browser, as discussed in "Browsing in iTunes." Choose **Edit**, **Hide Browser**.

PLAYING MUSIC ON AN iPOD

Current iPod models have five buttons and a click wheel to control playback and navigation.

Start

Scroll

Scroll

Press

Press

1 Press

1 With the iPod on (press any button) and displaying the main menu, plug earbuds into its headphone jack.

2 Move your finger counter-clockwise on the click wheel to select **Music** on the main menu.

3 Press the **Play/Pause** button to hear a tune.

4 Move your finger around the click wheel to adjust the volume.

Continued

TIP

Shuffle Play

You can also begin playing by selecting **Shuffle Songs** on the iPod's main menu, and then pressing **Play**. Items subject to shuffling include all songs, podcasts, and audiobooks currently stored on the iPod. See the "Shuffling Songs on an iPod" section later in this chapter for information about shuffling a single playlist.

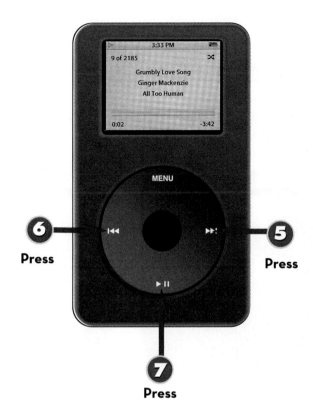

6 Press

5 Press

7 Press

5 Press the **Next** button to hear the next song, and then press **Next** again.

6 Press **Previous** to return to the second song. Pressing **Previous** twice goes back two songs.

7 Press **Play/Pause** again to stop playback.

End

TIP

Now Playing

To see what song is currently playing on an iPod with a display, scroll to the **Now Playing** item in the menu, and press the **center button**.

BROWSING MUSIC ON AN iPOD

Just like in iTunes, songs on your iPod are organized by artist, album, and genre.

Start

Press

Press

Press

Press

1 Press the **Menu** button to move up one level from your current position. Press it again if you don't see the main menu, labeled **iPod**.

2 Use the click wheel to move to the **Music** item, and press the **center button**.

3 Select **Artists** with the click wheel and press the **center button**. You see an alphabetical list of artists on your iPod.

4 Scroll through the list to an artist you like and press the **center button**. The iPod displays a list of all albums by that artist. The **All** item shows all songs by the artist.

Continued

— NOTE

More Categories

The Music menu also includes categories for songs, genres, and composers. Beneath the Genre and Composer categories, songs are organized by artist. The Songs category simply lists songs alphabetically.

Scroll

Press

Press

Press

5 Press the **center button** to see an album's contents.

6 Press **Play** to hear a song.

7 Press **Menu** until you reach the Music menu.

8 Use the click wheel to move to the **Albums** menu and press the **center button**. A list of albums appears. From here, you can browse each album's songs.

End

FAST FORWARD AND REWIND

You can move backward and forward within songs, using the Previous and Next buttons.

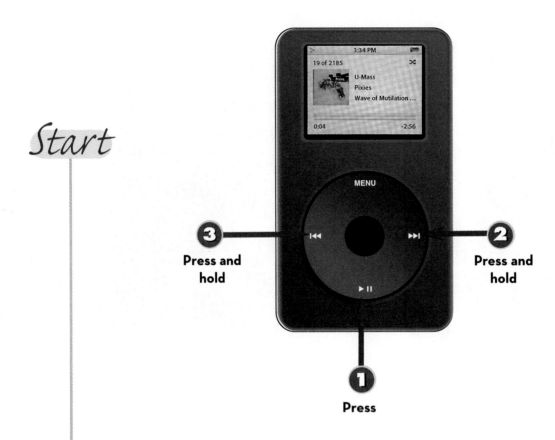

Start

3 Press and hold

2 Press and hold

1 Press

End

1 Begin playing a song on the iPod.

2 Press and hold the **Next** button. You'll hear the song skip forward as you hold down the button. Let go of the **Next** button to return to regular playback.

3 Press and hold the **Previous** button to go backward within the song, and release the button to hear the song normally.

CAUTION

Press Firmly

You might inadvertently move to the next song, rather than skipping through the current one, if you don't keep your finger firmly pressed on the **Previous** or **Next** button while rewinding or fast forwarding a song.

NAVIGATING PLAYLISTS ON AN iPOD

The iTunes playlists you've synchronized with your iPod or created exclusively for the iPod can be found in the Playlists menu. The iPod shuffle does not use playlists.

Start

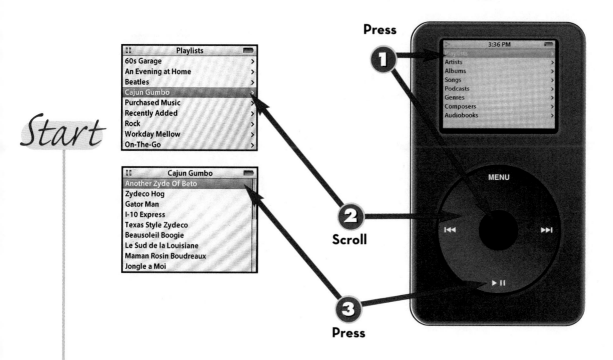

Press

Scroll

Press

1. Open the Playlists menu from the main menu by pressing the **center button**.

2. Scroll to a playlist you want to hear, and press the **center button**.

3. Press **Play** to hear a song from the playlist.

End

SHUFFLING SONGS ON AN iPOD

There are two ways to shuffle songs on an iPod or iPod nano: the Shuffle Songs command and the shuffle settings. Shuffle Songs begins playback immediately, shuffling all tracks on your iPod. Shuffle settings allow you to control how and whether music you are about to play is shuffled.

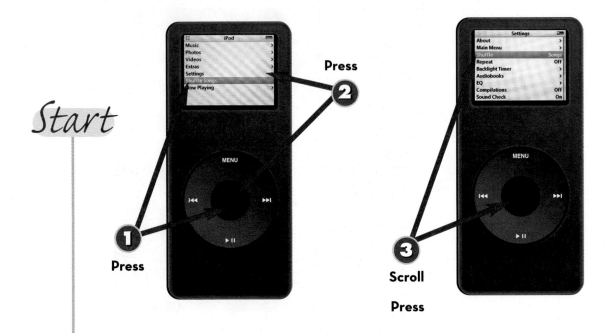

Start

Press

Press

Scroll

Press

① To shuffle all songs on the iPod, regardless of playlist, and to begin playing them immediately, choose **Shuffle Songs** from the main menu and press the **center button**.

② To shuffle the contents of a playlist or a group of songs you've browsed to, begin by choosing **Settings** from the main menu.

③ Scroll to **Shuffle** and press the **center button**. The shuffle setting changes from **Off** to **Songs**.

Continued

NOTE

Shuffle Icon
When you play shuffled songs, the shuffle icon appears below the title bar on the iPod.

4 Press   **5** Press

4 Press the **center button** again to shuffle by Albums, and then press the **Menu** button to return to the main menu.

5 Navigate to a music playlist and press **Play**. The songs play in random order.

End

NOTE

Shuffle Albums or Artists

The Shuffle option on the Setting menu not only works for playlists, but also for albums or collections of music by an artist. If you select **Shuffle, Songs** before browsing to an artist's name under the Artists menu, all songs by that artist are shuffled when you select **All** and press the **center button**.

CONTROLLING AN iPOD SHUFFLE

The iPod shuffle's controls are similar to those of the larger iPods. Because there is no display, there is no Menu button. A switch on the back turns the device on and off.

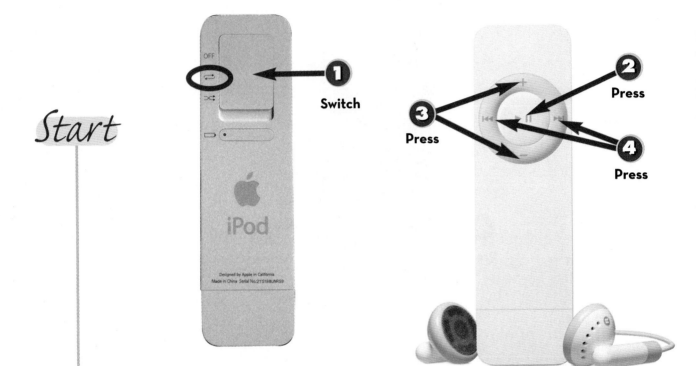

Start

Switch

2 Press

3 Press

4 Press

 Turn the shuffle on by moving the switch on the back downward, into the middle, **Play in Order** position. The status light on the front of the shuffle is activated.

2 Press **Play** to hear a song.

3 Use the **Volume Up** and **Volume Down** buttons to adjust the volume.

4 Press **Next** to move to the next song in the play order, and **Previous** to hear an earlier one.

 End

TIP
Start at the Top
To move to the beginning of the iPod shuffle playlist, quickly press the **Play** button three times.

TIP
Fast Forward
To move quickly through a playing song, hold down the **Next** or **Previous** button.

SHUFFLING SONGS ON AN iPOD SHUFFLE
The iPod shuffle has two modes: shuffle and play in order.

Start

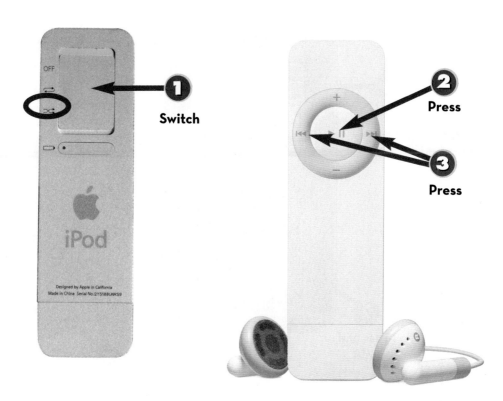

Switch

2
Press

3
Press

1 Move the switch on the back of the iPod shuffle down to the **Shuffle** position.

2 Press **Play** to hear a song.

3 Use the **Next** and **Previous** buttons to move through the shuffled playlist.

End

TIP
Fast Forward or Rewind
Holding down the **Previous** or **Next** buttons while a song
is playing skips backward or forward through the song.

CREATING AN ON-THE-GO PLAYLIST

Standard playlists are created in iTunes and copied to your iPod. An on-the-go playlist is a temporary playlist you create from items on an iPod.

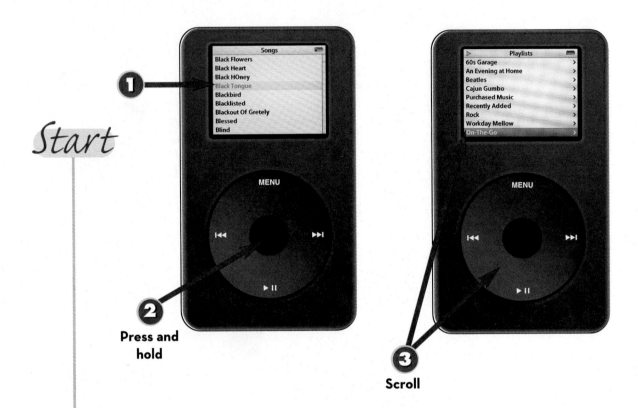

Start

Press and hold

Scroll

① Find a song on the iPod that you want to add to an on-the-go-playlist.

② Press and hold the **center button** for one second. The song title blinks and is added to the on-the-go playlist. Choose more songs to add to the on-the-go playlist by selecting each and pressing the **center button**.

③ To see the new on-the-go playlist, open the Playlists menu and scroll to **On-the-Go**.

Continued

TIP

On-the-Go in Bulk

To add all songs by an artist or a complete album to an on-the-go playlist, select the artist or album and hold down the **center button** to add the tracks to your playlist.

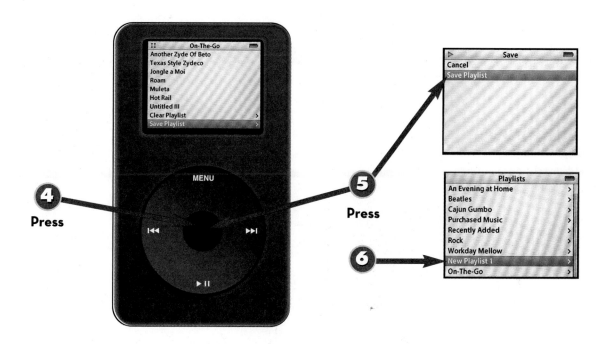

4 Press

5 Press

6

4 Press the **center button**. The songs you added appear in the on-the-go playlist. You can now play them just like any other iPod playlist.

5 To keep the contents of the playlist for later, scroll to **Save Playlist** and press the **center button**. Press again to confirm the save.

6 View the saved playlist by opening it in the **Playlists** menu.

End

TIP
Delete On-the-Go Lists
To remove all items from an on-the-go playlist, scroll to the bottom of the on-the-go playlist and choose **Clear Playlist**.

USING THE iPOD EQUALIZER

The iPod includes 22 equalizer presets you can use to affect the bass, treble, and midrange of your music.

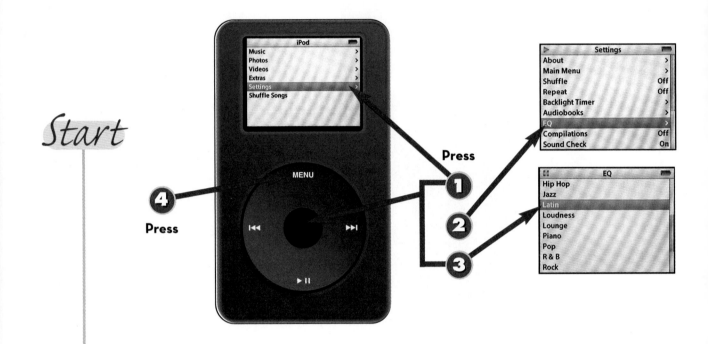

Start

Press

Press

① Choose **Settings** from the main **iPod** menu and press the **center button**.

② Select **EQ** and press the **center button**.

③ Choose one of the **EQ** presets from the list and press the **center button**.

④ Press the **Menu** button to leave the EQ menu and confirm the setting.

End

NOTE

Equalizer Eats Battery Power

If your iPod's battery is running low and you're not able to charge it, turn off the equalizer to conserve the battery.

USING SOUND CHECK

The iPod's Sound Check feature normalizes the volume of music you play so it isn't necessary to continually adjust the playback volume.

Start

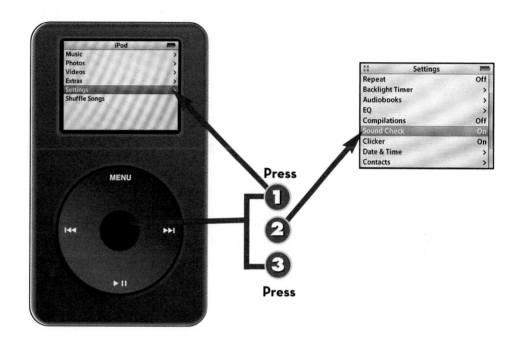

Press

Press

1 Choose **Settings** from the iPod's main menu and press the **center button**.

2 Choose **Sound Check** from the Settings menu and press the **center button**.

3 Press the **center button** to toggle Sound Check on or off.

End

FINDING AND LISTENING TO PODCASTS

Podcasts are downloadable audio programs to which you can subscribe using iTunes. Thousands of programs produced by publishers, TV networks, organizations, and individuals are available. Some podcasts are highly polished shows that sound much like traditional radio programs; National Public Radio is among the largest podcast producers. Others are homegrown efforts, created especially for the podcast medium, covering technology, business, music, sports, news, and comedy. There's a podcast for almost every interest.

Podcasters produce new episodes periodically, which iTunes automatically downloads into the Podcasts playlist. The iTunes Music Store includes a large directory of podcasts produced by individuals and big media organizations. You can browse or search for them, or add a podcast URL manually.

The Podcasts playlist keeps track of which shows you're subscribed to and which episodes you have downloaded. iTunes can then synchronize the Podcasts playlist with your iPod.

PODCAST DIRECTORY

Podcasts
source

Podcast search   Featured podcasts

Top podcasts

BROWSING THE PODCAST DIRECTORY

The Music Store's Podcast Directory lists thousands of podcasts. The Music Store features new podcasts frequently, and tracks those with the most subscribers.

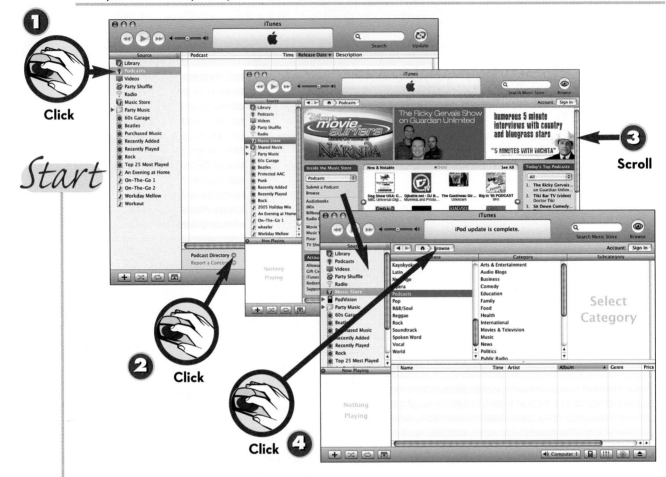

1 Click

Start

3 Scroll

2 Click

4 Click

1 In iTunes, click the **Podcasts** item in the source pane.

2 Click the button next to **Podcast Directory**.

3 Scroll the directory page to see all of the featured podcasts and categories. Click a link or image to learn more about the show.

4 Click **Browse** to see lists of podcasts organized by category.

End

TIP

Another Path
You can also reach the Podcasts Directory from the Music Store. Click **Music Store** and choose **Podcasts** from the Genre list.

SEARCHING FOR PODCASTS IN THE DIRECTORY

You can search for podcasts from the Podcasts directory or the iTunes search field.

Type

1

Start

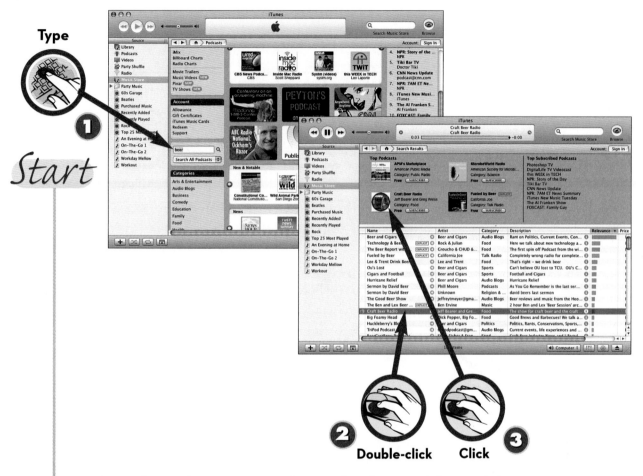

2 Double-click   Click **3**

1 In the Podcasts directory, type a keyword in the search box and then press **Enter**. iTunes searches for podcasts with names and keywords matching what you type.

2 To sample a podcast from the search results you receive, double-click it.

3 To see a full page of information about the podcast, including all available episodes, click the image to the left of the podcast's name.

End

NOTE

Explicit Content

Podcasts with adult content are often, but not always, labeled with the Explicit tag next to their names. In many cases, the podcast producer has given the show this label, though Apple also adds the tag based on keywords or content. Parents should proceed with caution.

TIP

Narrow Your Search

To limit your podcast search to the name or author, choose your preferred option from the drop-down menu below the podcast search field.

SUBSCRIBING TO A PODCAST FROM THE DIRECTORY

Subscribing to a podcast adds it to your Podcasts playlist, downloads the most recent program, and watches for and downloads new episodes when they are published.

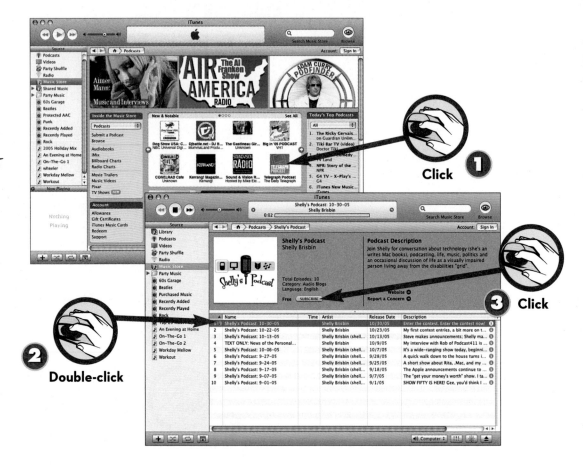

Start

Click ❶

Double-click ❷

Click ❸

❶ In the podcast directory, choose a podcast you would like to hear by clicking its link or icon. Information about the podcast appears, including links to its episodes.

❷ Double-click an episode to sample the podcast. You hear a minute or two of the program.

❸ Click **Subscribe** to subscribe to the podcast.

Continued

NOTE

Control Downloads

The next task, "Customizing Podcast Download Settings," describes how to change podcast download settings. If you don't want to download the most recent show from a podcast you've just subscribed to, read and follow these steps before subscribing.

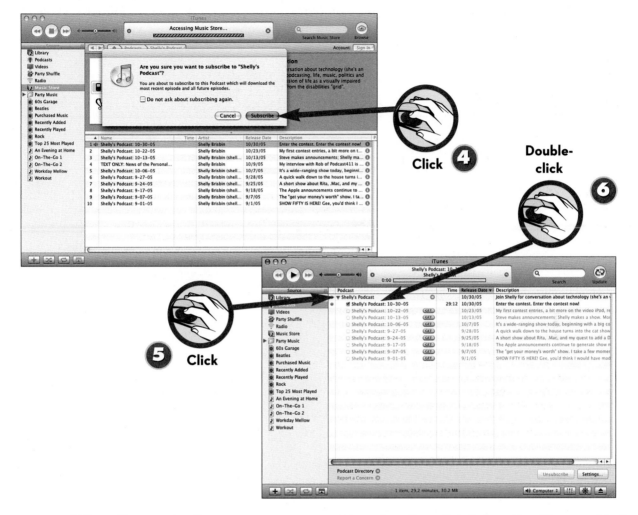

Click ④

Double-click ⑥

⑤ **Click**

④ When iTunes asks if you are sure you want to subscribe, click **Subscribe**. iTunes adds the podcast and takes you to the podcast's source, downloading the most recent episode of the podcast.

⑤ Click the **expansion triangle** next to the podcast name to see the episode that is being downloaded, as well as older shows. When the download is complete, the new episode appears with a bullet indicating that is has not yet been played.

⑥ To hear it, double-click the downloaded show, or select it and press the **Play** button.

End

TIP

Get More Episodes

If the podcast you've subscribed to has additional episodes available, their dimmed titles appear under the show's title. Click the **Get** button next to any additional episode to download it.

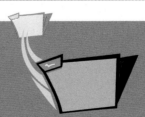

CUSTOMIZING PODCAST DOWNLOAD SETTINGS

By default, subscribing to a podcast downloads the most recent episode. iTunes checks for new podcasts once per day. You can change these preferences to suit your needs.

Click ①

Start

② **Click**

① Click the **Podcasts** item in the source pane.

② Click the **Settings** button.

Continued

TIP

Update When Needed

If you want to check the status of a podcast between regularly scheduled updates, you can force an update to an individual podcast. Right-click (Windows) or Control-click (Mac) the podcast title and choose **Update Podcast**. iTunes downloads any new episodes it finds.

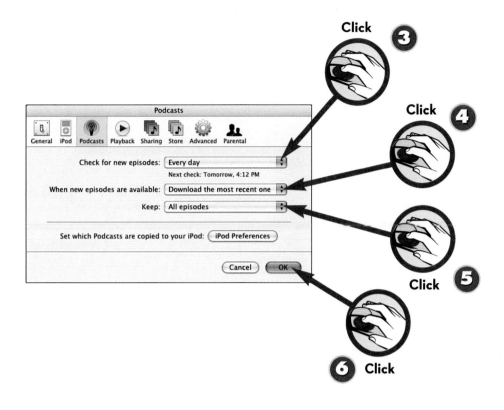

Click ③

Click ④

Click ⑤

⑥ **Click**

③ Choose how often iTunes checks for new episodes of podcasts you subscribed to from the **Check for New Episodes** menu.

④ Tell iTunes how to handle new episodes by making a choice from the **When New Episodes Are Available** menu.

⑤ Use the **Keep** menu to tell iTunes how to handle podcast episodes that have not yet been played.

⑥ Click **OK**.

End

TIP
Update When Broken
iTunes occasionally has trouble communicating with a podcast site. If you see a bullet with an exclamation point next to a podcast in your Podcasts playlist, you can recheck for new shows by right-clicking (Windows) or Control-clicking (Mac) on the affected podcast, and choosing **Update Podcast** from the menu.

SUBSCRIBING TO PODCASTS FROM THE WEB

Most podcasters offer a website where you can subscribe to or learn more about the show. Many offer a direct link that adds your show to iTunes.

Type 1

Start

Click 2

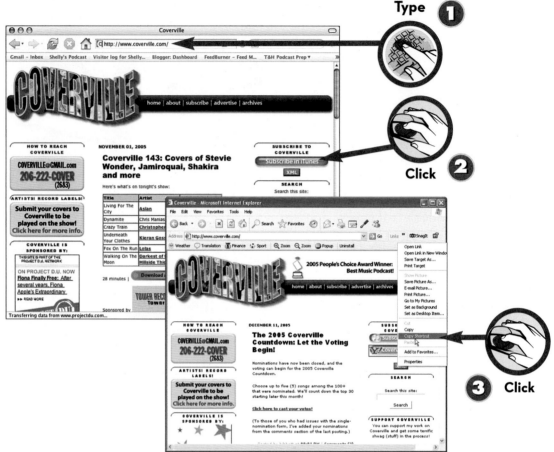

Click 3

1. Go to a podcaster's website, or find a podcast at a directory site such as www. podcastpickle.com.
2. On the podcast site, locate and click the **iTunes subscription badge** or **link**. iTunes should open and your podcast should be added.
3. If the site has a Subscribe link that doesn't say iTunes, right-click (Windows) or Control-click (Mac) on the Subscribe link, and choose to copy the link to your clipboard.

Continued

NOTE

Where's the XML?

Podcasters use a variety of badges to link to their podcast feeds. If you don't see the XML badge shown on this page, look for one that says Feed, Subscribe, or RSS.

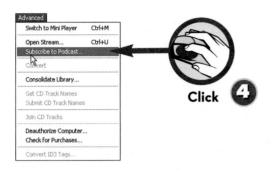

Click ④

Click ⑤

④ In iTunes, choose **Advanced, Subscribe to Podcast**.

⑤ Paste the link into the field that appears, and then click **OK**. iTunes adds the podcast and downloads episodes according to your preferences.

End

NOTE

Glitchy iTunes

Clicking on a subscribe via iTunes link should open iTunes and take you to the podcast's subscription page. If it doesn't, try opening iTunes and clicking on the podcaster's iTunes link again. Sometimes it's just the kick iTunes needs.

ADDING PODCASTS TO AN iPOD SHUFFLE

There is no automatic way to synchronize the Podcasts playlist in iTunes with the iPod shuffle. You can copy podcasts to the shuffle manually, however.

2 Click

3 Click

Start

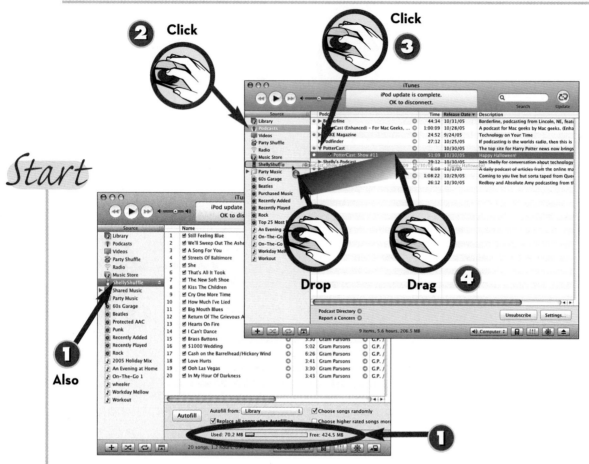

Drop **Drag** **4**

1

Also

1 Connect an iPod shuffle to your computer and select it in iTunes. Note how much space remains on the device.

2 Click the **Podcasts** item in the iTunes source pane.

3 Click the **expansion triangle** next to a podcast to see episodes that have been downloaded to your computer. Unplayed episodes have a blue dot next to them.

4 Drag an episode onto the iPod shuffle's icon to copy it.

End

TIP

Deleting from the Shuffle

To delete one or more items from the iPod shuffle, making room for podcasts, simply select the item in the Shuffle playlist and press **Delete**.

TIP

Save Space

Podcast files are larger than music files. To shrink high-bit rate podcasts and store the maximum number of items on the shuffle, open **Preferences** in iTunes, choose **iPod**, and check the **Convert Higher Bit Rate Songs to 128 Kbps AAC for This iPod** option.

ADDING PODCASTS TO AN iPOD

Like music playlists, podcasts in iTunes can be synchronized with your iPod. iTunes provides specific preferences for podcast syncing, allowing you to sync some or all podcasts.

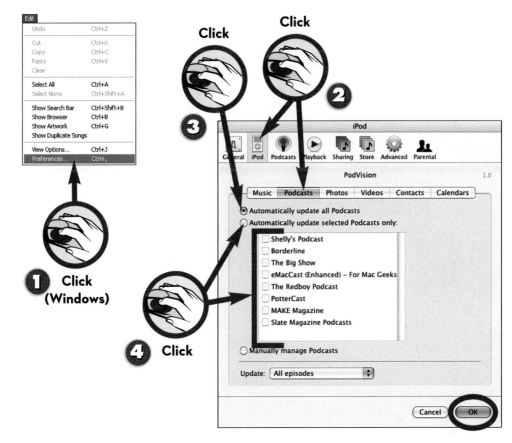

Start

1 Click
(Windows)

When you have subscribed to several podcasts in iTunes, connect your iPod and choose **Edit**, **Preferences** (Windows) or **iTunes**, **Preferences** (Mac).

2 Click the **iPod** tab and then click **Podcasts**.

3 Click the **Automatically Update All Podcasts** option to do just that.

4 To update individual podcasts instead, click **Automatically Update Selected Podcasts Only**, and click the check boxes for those you want on your iPod. Click **OK**.

End

NOTE

Separate but Equal

The preferences you set for iPod updating are completely separate from those used to update music playlists, so you can update all podcasts while updating only some music playlists, or vice versa.

PLAYING ENHANCED PODCASTS IN iTUNES

Enhanced podcasts are organized into chapters, allowing you to navigate directly to a particular point in the podcast, and, when listening in iTunes, to go directly to web links associated with individual sections of the enhanced podcast.

Double-click

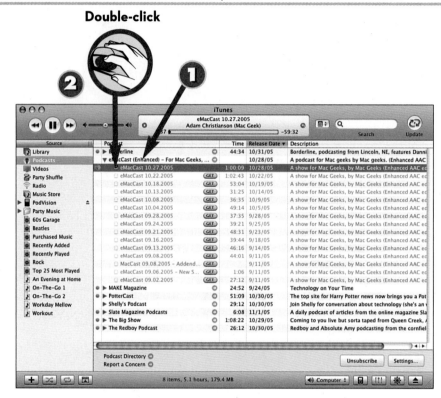

1 Subscribe to an enhanced podcast and download an episode to your computer. We'll use the eMacCast (search for it in the iTunes Podcast directory) as an example.

2 Double-click an episode of the enhanced podcast to play it.

Continued

Click

Click

5

Click

4

3 Choose an item from the **Chapters** menu. The podcast skips to the beginning of the chapter you've chosen. Repeat the command to select a different chapter.

4 If it's not already visible, click **Show/Hide Artwork**. The chapter images appear in the artwork pane.

5 Click inside the artwork pane. If the chapter is linked to a web page or podcast, you are taken there. (Not all enhanced podcasts have links.)

End

PLAYING PODCASTS ON AN iPOD

When you tell iTunes to synchronize your podcast subscriptions with an iPod, a Podcasts playlist is added to the iPod.

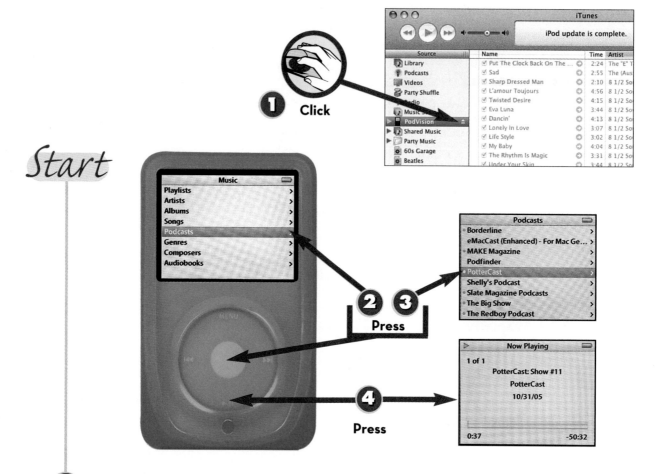

Start

1 Click

2 **3** Press

4 Press

1 Synchronize your iPod and eject the iPod from your computer.

2 Choose **Music** from the iPod's main menu, and then **Podcasts**.

3 Select a podcast and press the **center button** to see its episodes.

4 Press **Play** to hear the episode.

Continued

TIP
Play Shortcut
If a podcast on your iPod has only one episode, pressing the **center button** with the show selected begins playback of the episode.

NOTE
Skins That Rock
If you like the look of the evo3 case seen in this task, check out these skins and many other cool accessories for your iPod at http://iskin.com.

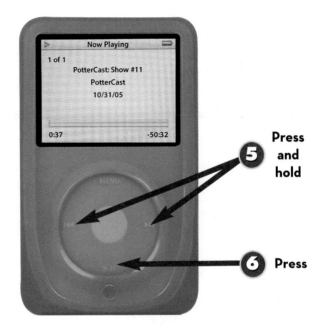

5 Press and hold

6 Press

5 Use the **Next** and **Previous** buttons (hold the button down) to move quickly through a podcast as it plays.

6 Press **Play/Stop** to quit listening to a podcast. Because podcasts downloaded by iTunes are converted into bookmarkable files, you can return to a podcast you haven't finished at a later time without losing your place.

End

TIP
Show Notes
Some podcasters include text-based show notes with their audio files. To view a podcaster's show notes, press the **center button** two or three times (depending on whether the podcast has artwork) while the show is playing. Use the click wheel to scroll through the show notes. You can press the **center button** again to view the default screen for this podcast again, or simply wait for the default screen to return automatically.

PLAYING ENHANCED PODCASTS ON AN iPOD

Just as they do in iTunes, enhanced podcasts' chapters allow you to move through a show on your iPod, one section at a time.

Start

1 Press

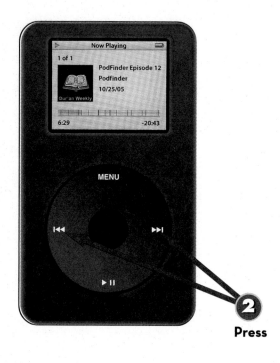

2 Press

1 Select an enhanced podcast on your iPod and press **Play**.

2 Press **Next** to move to the next chapter. Press **Previous** to move back one section. The iPod display skips ahead to update the time, and shows the chapter's artwork, if any.

End

─ NOTE ─
Spotting Enhanced Podcasts
You can tell a podcast playing on your iPod is enhanced by the hashmarks that appear on the progress bar as the podcast plays. Each hashmark represents a chapter.

MAINTAINING AND UNSUBSCRIBING

Depending on the podcast settings you've chosen, you might want to manually delete individual episodes of podcasts. You might also decide to unsubscribe from the podcast at some point.

Click ②

① **Click**

Start

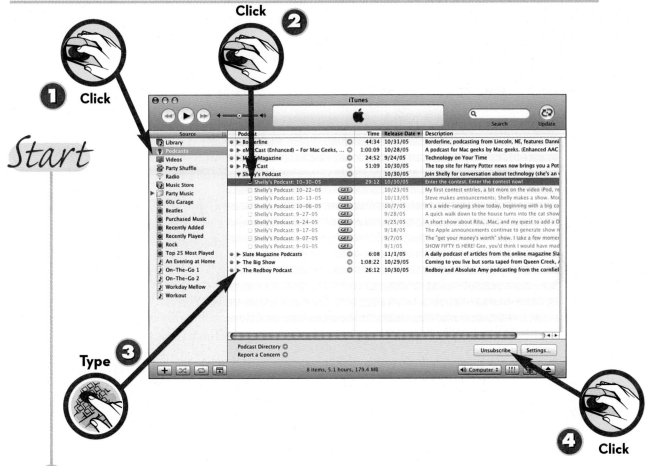

Type ③

Unsubscribe ④ **Click**

① Select the **Podcasts** item in the iTunes source pane.

② Open a podcast listing and select an episode that has been downloaded and played.

③ To delete the episode from the music library, press **Delete**. To delete the podcast file from your computer, press ⌘**+Option+Delete** (Mac) or **Ctrl+Delete** (Windows).

④ To unsubscribe from a podcast without removing previously downloaded episodes, select the podcast item and click **Unsubscribe**.

End

NOTE
Clean House
Podcast episodes are stored in the Podcasts folder, inside the iTunes Music folder. To be sure old podcasts are deleted, clear them from this folder. On the Mac, the path is *username*/Music/iTunes/iTunes Music/Podcast. In Windows, the path is \My Documents\My Music\iTunes\iTunes Music\Podcasts.

TIP
Remove All
To unsubscribe from a podcast and remove all episodes, select the podcast and choose **Edit**, **Clear**.

WATCHING VIDEOS IN iTUNES AND ON YOUR iPOD

Although iTunes is primarily a music and audio tool, you can use it to download and play video programs, as long as the programs are in a compatible format, such as QuickTime, MPEG-4, or H.264. You can watch videos in a small window within iTunes, or view them using your computer's full screen.

iTunes supports video formats including QuickTime and MPEG-4 (video files with **.mov**, **.m4v**, or **.mp4** file extensions that are viewable in QuickTime Player). The fifth generation iPods are the first and only members of the iPod family to support video playback. You can play MPEG-4 and H.264 video files, as long as they have been encoded for the iPod's screen size and resolution. The iTunes Music Store sells TV episodes and music videos that are designed for iPod playback, and some podcasters are now using video. You can convert other video files for iPod playback using Apple's QuickTime Pro software.

iPod video syncing works much like music or podcast syncing. Downloaded videos are added to a special playlist called Videos. It's replicated on your iPod when you choose to sync the two. You can create playlists for videos in iTunes, and you can use one of several built-in iPod video playlists to keep your programs organized.

A 60GB iPod can hold 150 hours of video programming, but be aware that the battery only lasts 1–3 hours when playing video.

PURCHASE VIDEOS FROM THE MUSIC STORE

DOWNLOADING VIDEO FROM THE iTUNES MUSIC STORE

The iTunes Music Store offers downloadable TV shows, music videos, and movie trailers. Many programs are available for $1.99.

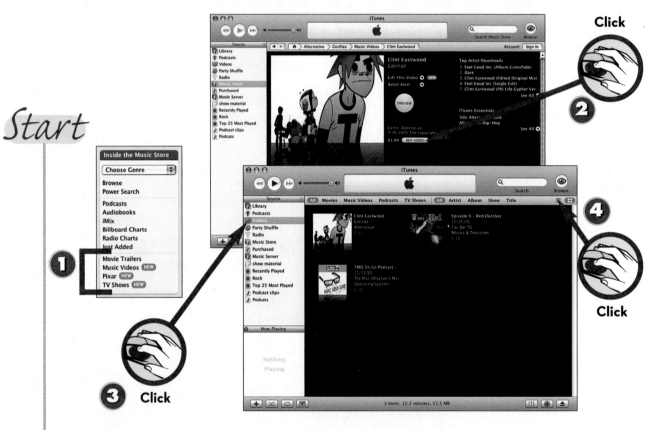

Start

Click

Click

Click

1. In iTunes, open the Music Store and click **Music Videos**, **Pixar**, or **TV Shows** to see programs you can buy.

2. Navigate to an individual episode or video and click **Buy Video**. iTunes completes the purchase and downloads your purchase.

3. Click **Videos** to see an image preview of each video in your library.

4. To see a list of videos instead of the preview images, click the **List View** button.

End

NOTE

Movie Trailers

Although the iTunes Music Store includes a section for movie trailers, these are not downloadable to an iPod. When you click a link to play a trailer, it appears within iTunes. Many movie companies provide links to trailers in several sizes, but they are not iPod-compatible.

FINDING MORE VIDEOS

The quickest way to find more iPod-compatible videos is to browse or search the Podcasts section of the Music Store. A number of podcasters have switched to or added video to their programs.

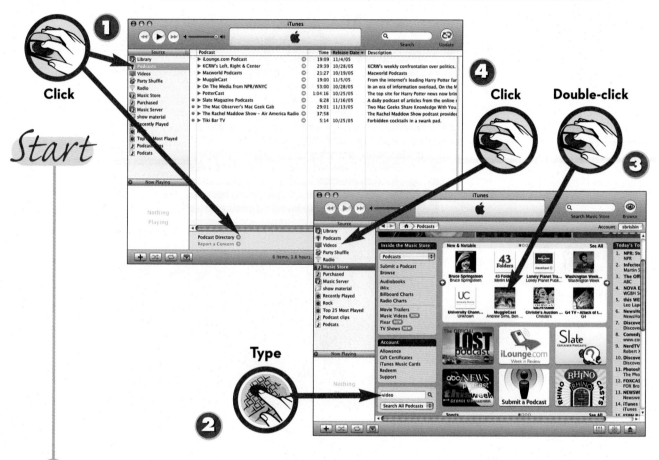

Click

Start

Type

Click   **Double-click**

1 In iTunes, click **Podcasts** and then **Podcast Directory**.

2 Scroll to the Search box, type **video**, and then press **Enter**. Video podcasts and podcasts related to *video* appear.

3 Locate a show you would want to see and double-click an episode to preview it, or click **Subscribe** to receive each episode as it is released. The first one begins downloading.

4 Click the **Videos** playlist to see videos that have been downloaded.

End

CAUTION

iPod Compatible or Not

All videos you download via iTunes aren't necessarily iPod-ready. If you can see a preview of the video in iTunes, you can rest assured that it *will* play on a fifth-generation iPod.

NOTE

See Yourself

You can also import your own video into iTunes. To view it on an iPod, you need to encode it for the iPod, as described in "Converting Your Videos for iPod Playback," later in this chapter.

PLAYING VIDEO IN iTUNES

Videos you download with iTunes appear in the Videos playlist. You'll also find them in the iTunes library, with a video icon. You can play an iTunes video in a small window within iTunes, or view it full screen.

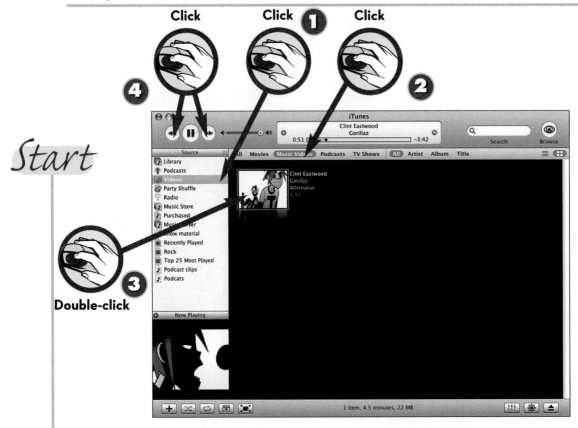

Start

Click ④

Click ①

Click ②

Double-click ③

1 Click **Videos** in the iTunes source pane. Previews of your videos appear.

2 Click a category in the **Search** bar to see only those kinds of videos.

3 Double-click a video to play it in the artwork/video pane.

4 Click the **Previous** or **Next** buttons to rewind or fast forward through the video.

Continued

 TIP

Another Way to Locate Videos

Videos in your iTunes library appear with a video icon in the main library listing. Video podcast files appear in the Podcasts playlist as well. Double-click any item with a video icon to play the video.

Double-click

⑤ Click

⑤ Double-click a video in the **Videos** playlist to begin playback.

⑥ Click the **Video** button to play the video full screen. Press **Esc** to return to iTunes.

End

─TIP─
Bookmarking Videos
Videos and podcasts you download through iTunes can be bookmarked so that when you stop video playback and resume it later, the video begins playing where you left off. Select the video in iTunes and open its Info window. Click the **Options** tab and check **Remember Play Position**.

ADDING VIDEO TO AN iPOD

After you have downloaded iPod-compatible videos to iTunes, you can add them to your iPod.

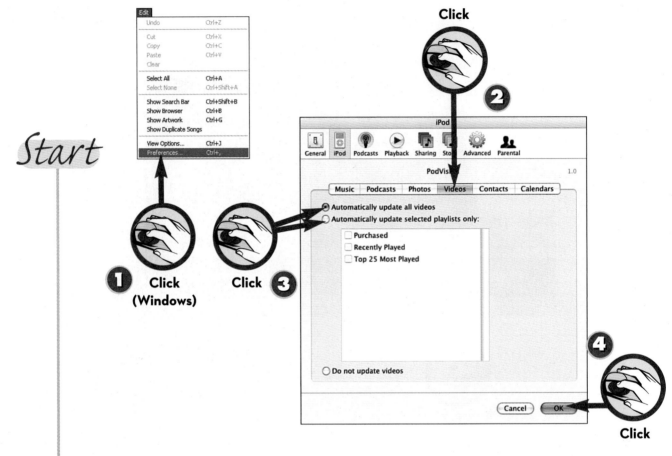

Start

Click

**Click
(Windows)**

Click

Click

1 With a video-compatible iPod connected to your computer, choose **iTunes**, **Preferences** (Mac), or **Edit**, **Preferences** (Windows) and click the **iPod** tab.

2 Click **Videos**.

3 Click **Automatically Update All Videos**, or click **Automatically Update Selected Playlists Only** to choose specific items.

4 Click **OK** to finish configuring iPod video access.

End

-TIP-
Which Playlists?
To be sure you get video podcasts, sync the podcast feed in Podcasts Preferences, or choose to sync all podcasts (as described in "Adding Podcasts to an iPod" in Part 8). Between the Videos and Podcasts syncing tabs, you get all iPod-compatible videos when you sync.

— NOTE —
Video Playlists Only
For the Automatically Update Selected Playlists Only option to add videos to your iPod, the playlists that you choose under that option have to contain videos.

MANAGING VIDEOS ON AN iPOD

Video-compatible iPods include three built-in playlists. You can also create your own video playlists and play videos from music or podcast playlists that include videos.

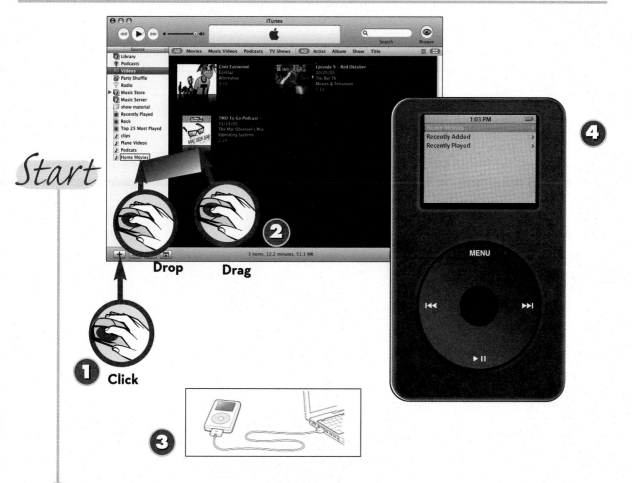

Start

Drop **Drag**

2

1 Click

3

4

1 In iTunes, click the **Create a Playlist** button to add a new playlist. Name the playlist.

2 Click the **Videos** playlist and drag one or more videos onto the new playlist.

3 Connect a video-compatible iPod to your computer to sync the two.

4 Disconnect the iPod and choose the **Videos** menu, and then the **Video Playlist** menu. Your new playlist appears on the iPod, along with all other regular or smart playlists containing at least one video.

End

NOTE

Confusing or Thorough?
Because any playlist with at least one video appears on your iPod's Video Playlists menu, you'll often see non-video items as well. For example, a recently played video appears in the Recently Played playlist when your iPod is synced.

TIP

Manage Your Own Playlists
If you sync individual playlists to your iPod rather than automatically adding everything, you can manage video playlists by setting which playlists are synced under the **Video** tab in iTunes's **iPod Preferences**.

PLAYING VIDEOS ON AN iPOD

Videos downloaded to your iPod appear in the Videos playlist. If your iPod doesn't support video, you won't see this playlist. Within Videos are category playlists for your videos.

Start

Press

Press

1 With your iPod disconnected from the computer, choose **Videos** from the main menu and press the **center button**.

2 Choose one of the three video categories: **Movies**, **Music Videos**, or **Video Podcasts**. The playlist where your video appears is determined by the genre associated with each file in iTunes.

Continued

— **NOTE** —

iPod Video Bookmarks

If you have used the **Remember Play Position** option in iTunes for a video that has been copied to your iPod, the iPod remembers those bookmark settings.

4

**Press and
hold**

MENU

3

Press

3 Select a video and press **Play**. The iPod fades to black and loads the video.

4 Press and hold down the **Previous** or **Next** button to rewind or fast forward through the
video.

End

TIP

Elapsed Time
To see how much time remains while a video is playing,
press the **center button** on your iPod.

PLAYING iPOD VIDEOS ON A TELEVISION

With an Apple iPod AV Cable ($19), you can play iPod videos on a television.

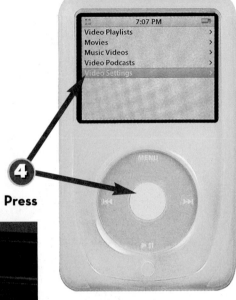

| 7:07 PM |
| Video Playlists > |
| Movies > |
| Music Videos > |
| Video Podcasts > |
| Video Settings |

Press

Start

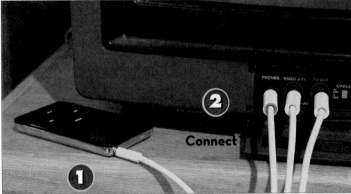

② **Connect**

① **Connect**

Connect

① Connect an Apple iPod AV cable to the headphone port of a video-compatible iPod.

② Connect the one video and two audio connectors to your television's RCA ports.

③ Be sure the television is set to receive a signal from the video ports you're using.

④ From the iPod's **Videos** menu, choose **Video Settings** and press the **center button**.

Continued

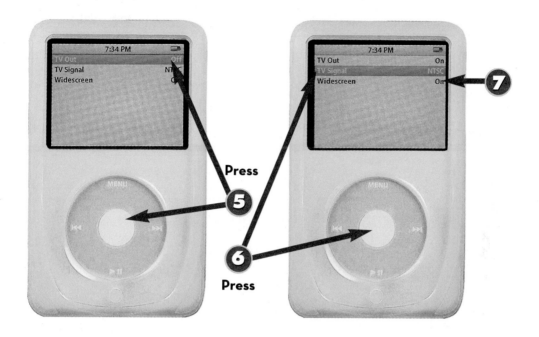

Press

5

6

Press

7

5 Select **TV Out** and press the **center button** to turn on this option.

6 If you are in the United States, be sure the **TV Signal** option is set to **NTSC**. Choose **PAL** in Europe.

7 If the television picture's aspect ratio looks wrong to you, turn on or off the iPod's **Widescreen** option.

End

NOTE

Skins and Stuff

Find more skins and cases like the one seen here by going to http://iskin.com.

CONVERTING YOUR VIDEOS FOR iPOD PLAYBACK ON A MAC

To play on an iPod, a video must be in a compatible format—MPEG-4 or H.264—and be encoded at a resolution of 320×240. If you have a Mac, you can encode videos for iPod with QuickTime Pro ($29) or another software tool, such as the $10 Podner.

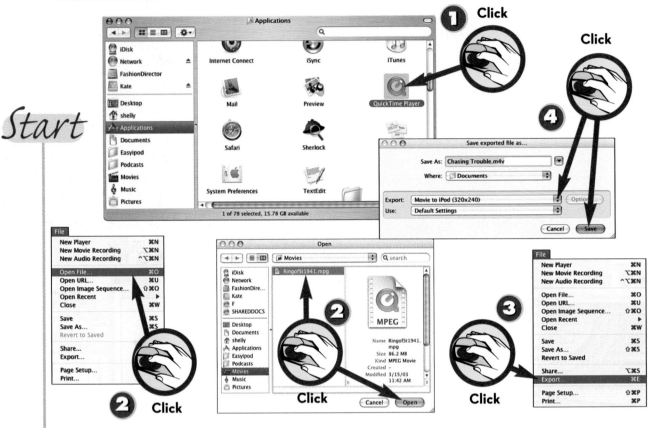

Start

1. Be sure that you have at least QuickTime 7.0.3 and QuickTime Pro installed, and launch the QuickTime Player application (QuickTime Pro adds menu options to QuickTime Player).

2. Choose **File**, **Open File**, and locate the video you want to convert. Click **Open**.

3. Choose **File**, **Export**.

4. Choose **Movie to iPod** from the Export drop-down menu and click **Save**.

Continued

TIP

A Free Video Conversion Option

If you don't have QuickTime Pro installed and don't want to buy it, try Podner ($10, www.splasm.com/products/productpodner.html).

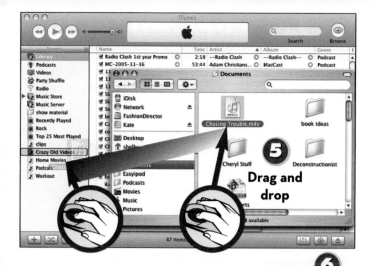

Drag and drop

5 Launch iTunes and drag the converted file onto the Library or a playlist. If you sync your iPod to specific iTunes playlists, be sure you add the movie to a playlist the iPod copies.

6 Connect a video-compatible iPod to your computer to sync the two.

7 When syncing is complete, unmount the iPod and locate your video under the iPod's Videos playlist.

End

TIP
More Ways to Export
With QuickTime Pro installed, you can use the **Share** command to export movies to your iPod from Apple's iMovie software for the Mac.

CONVERTING YOUR VIDEOS FOR iPOD PLAYBACK ON A WINDOWS COMPUTER

QuickTime Pro is available from Apple for Windows, and can be used to convert videos for playback on an iPod. Another option is the free Videora iPod Converter (www.videora.com). Videora iPod Converter supports standard Windows formats, including AVI and MPEG.

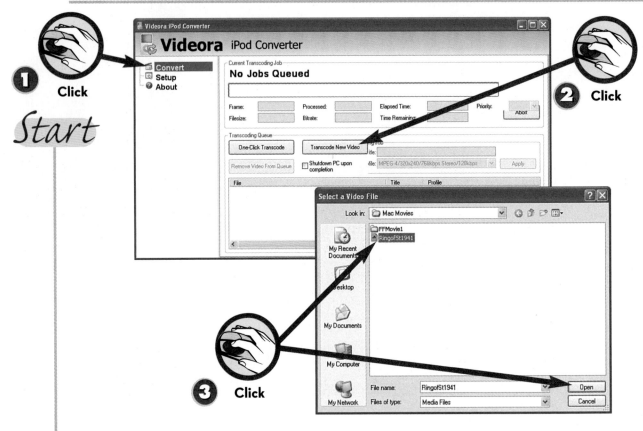

1 In Videora iPod Converter, click **Convert**.

2 Click **Transcode New Video**.

3 Navigate to the movie you want to convert and click **Open**. Videora displays the movie's name and file type. You can change the name of the movie if you want.

Continued

TIP

Find Your Videos

To choose an easily accessible folder for videos you convert with Videora iPod Converter, click **Setup**, and then click the **Browse** button next to the Output Videos To label. Navigate to your favorite folder and click **OK**. When you complete video conversion, the iPod-compatible movies are saved here.

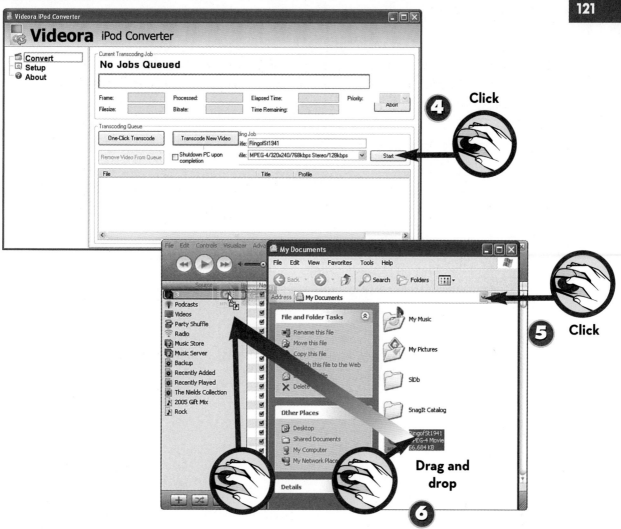

Click 4

Click 5

Drag and drop 6

4 Click **Start**. Videora encodes your movie for iPod playback. This might take some time.

5 When the conversion is complete, switch to Windows Explorer and locate the folder containing your converted video.

6 Drag the video into the iTunes library.

End

TIP

DVD Conversion

Videora iPod Converter is a sister application to Videora, which can convert DVD movies into a format you can play on your iPod.

part 10

LISTENING TO AUDIOBOOKS

The iPod is a natural for audiobooks, whether you listen on the train, in the car, or on the treadmill. The iTunes Music Store and Audible.com are the largest sources of audiobooks, and their tools and file formats are designed to work best with iPods.

You can find all types of audio books here from novels to books for kids. Take some time to browse around and see all of the options available both on iTunes and Audible.com.

In this chapter, you'll learn how to find audiobooks and how to make the most of them in iTunes and on the iPod. You'll also learn how to import audiobooks from CDs into iTunes.

AUDIOBOOKS AT THE iTUNES MUSIC STORE

Featured books

Genre features

Best sellers

BUYING AUDIOBOOKS AT THE iTUNES MUSIC STORE

The iTunes Music Store has partnered with Audible.com to offer a wide selection of audio-book titles. The Music Store does not stock the full Audible.com library, but you will find Music Store–exclusive audiobooks.

Start

Type

Click

Click

3

1 In iTunes, open the Music Store and click **Audiobooks**.

2 Use the featured selections, the top audiobooks list, and book genre categories (you will probably need to scroll to see these) to find books that interest you.

3 Search by author, title, or keyword using the iTunes search field (unlike Music and Podcast sections, there is no dedicated search field on the Audiobooks page).

Continued

TIP

Narrow Your Search

Because your audiobook search looks throughout the iTunes Music Store, you might want to click the **Audiobooks** button on the Search bar to limit your results to audiobooks. You'll see the search bar above the Music Store after you have performed a search.

TIP

Organize Your Books

It's a good idea to create a playlist for audio-books you download from iTunes or else-where. You can create a smart playlist that finds files with the audiobooks genre.

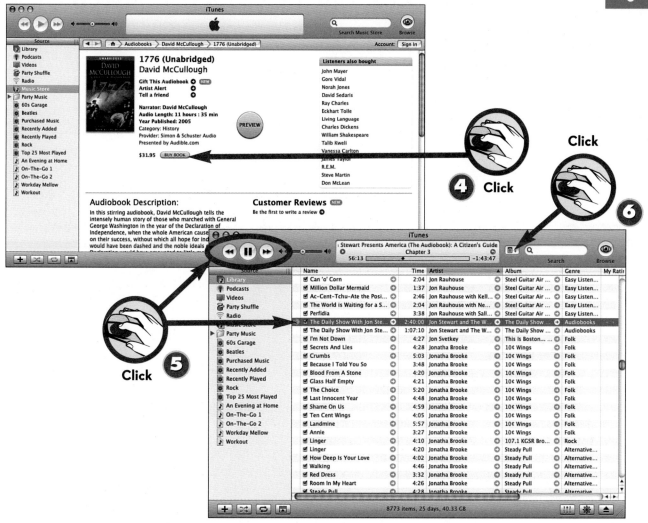

4 When you find an audiobook you'd like to buy, click **Buy Book**. The book is downloaded to your music library and added to the Purchased Music playlist under the Music Store item.

5 Select the book file in your music library and use the **Play/Stop**, **Previous**, and **Next** buttons to navigate it.

6 If the book has chapter divisions, use the **Chapters** menu to skip forward or backward.

End

NOTE

Save Your Place

Audiobooks from the iTunes Music Store and Audible.com typically consist of one or two very long audio files. Chances are that you will not listen to the entire book in one sitting. Fortunately, audiobooks are supplied in a bookmarkable format, meaning that if you stop playback and return to the book later, iTunes begins playing exactly where you left off.

RIPPING AUDIOBOOK CDS TO YOUR COMPUTER

Ripping audiobooks from CD to iTunes is much like ripping music CDs. The main difference is the need to keep audiobook files organized so they can be played in order.

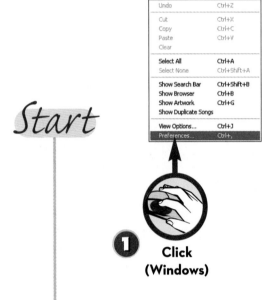

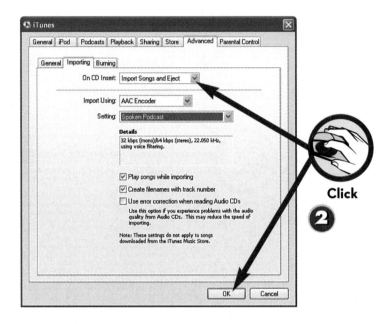

Start

1 Click
(Windows)

2 Click

1 If you don't have iTunes set to automatically import CDs when you insert them, choose **iTunes**, **Preferences** (Mac) or **Edit**, **Preferences** (Windows); click the **Advanced** tab and then click **Importing**.

2 Click **Import Songs and Eject** from the On CD Insert menu and click **OK**.

3 Insert the first CD of an audiobook you want to rip. iTunes imports the files and ejects the CD when it's finished.

Continued

TIP

Ripping Format

You can rip audiobooks in any of iTunes's audio formats by choosing one from the Import Using menu in iTunes's Importing Preferences window. The best choices are MP3 or AAC because these are highly compressed. If you don't have an iPod and intend to copy audiobook files to some other audio player, choose MP3. AAC is a higher-quality format, and is compatible with all iPods.

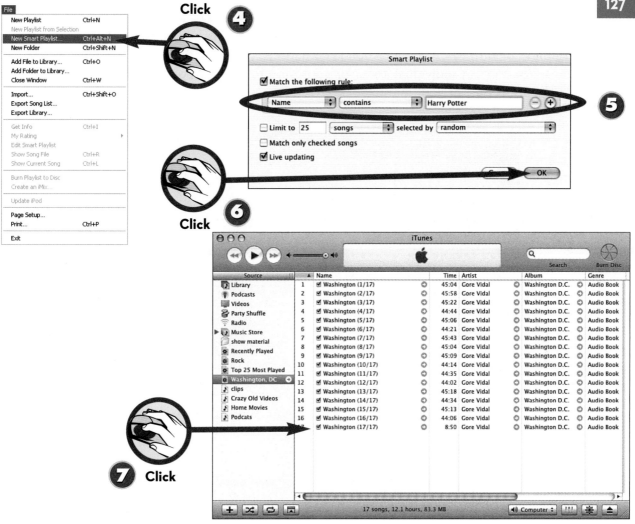

4 Choose **File, New Smart Playlist**.

5 Add criteria to the smart playlist that matches the book's name and/or author. Make the criteria narrow enough to eliminate items that are not part of the book you're importing.

6 Click **OK** to finish the playlist. As you import new book files, they are added to the music library and your new smart playlist.

7 When all of the CDs have been imported, check the smart playlist to make sure that all of the files are included and that there are no extras. Edit the smart playlist if necessary.

End

TIP
Make Things Consistent
Some publishers don't do a very good job of creating consistent ID3 tags for audiobook files. This makes it tough to keep downloaded books organized within a smart playlist. To give all files associated with a book a common set of criteria, select all of the files and press ⌘+I (Mac) or **Ctrl+I** (Windows). Type the book's title in the Album field, and choose **Audiobooks** from the Genre menu. Use identical criteria for your smart playlist.

BUYING AUDIOBOOKS FROM AUDIBLE.COM

Audible.com sells a wide array of audio programs, including books, periodicals, and radio programs. When you download Audible.com items, you can add them automatically to iTunes. You can buy individual items, or subscribe to Audible.com and download one or more items as part of your monthly subscription.

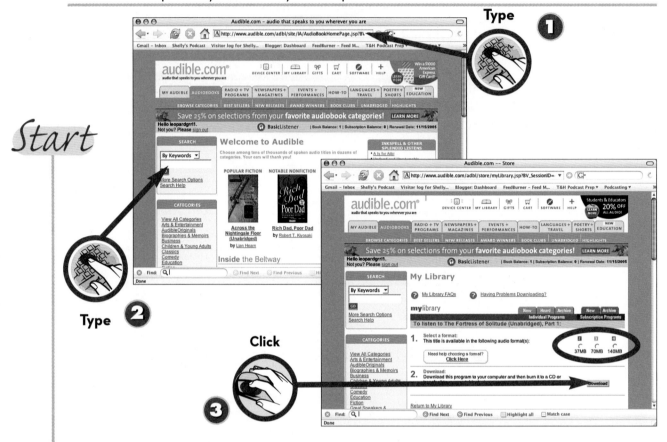

Start

Type 1

Type 2

Click 3

1. Go to www.audible.com. If you don't already have an Audible.com account, create one. Note that some Audible.com accounts offer premiums, such as a free iPod shuffle.

2. Search for a book or other item you want to buy and complete the purchase.

3. Audible.com takes you to your library, where you can download your purchase. You are asked to choose one of several formats with varying sizes and audio quality. Your web browser begins the download when you click **OK**.

4. When the file has been downloaded, it is added to your iTunes library and begins playing.

End

TIP

Audible Formats

Audible.com's four audio formats provide increasing levels of quality (1 sounds like a telephone and produces very small files; 4 is MP3-like, but generates bigger files). You must choose format 2, 3, or 4 to play Audible.com files on an iPod. Format 1 is not supported at all on the Macintosh.

ADDING AUDIOBOOKS TO AN iPOD

When you add audiobooks from Audible.com or the iTunes Music Store to an iPod, they are added to the Audiobooks playlist. You can't force ripped audiobooks into the Audiobooks playlist, so you need to sync your own iTunes playlist to the iPod.

Start

Click ❶

❶ If you synchronize your music library with an iPod, Control+click (Mac) or right-click (Windows) the **iPod** playlist in iTunes, and choose **Update** to add books you have recently added to your library.

❷ If you synchronize specific playlists to your iPod, add those containing audiobooks in iTunes's iPod Preferences. If you manage your iPod manually, drag audiobook files onto the iPod item.

End

TIP

Auto Audiobooks

However you synchronize your iPod, any audiobook file from the iTunes Music Store or Audible.com added to your iPod is included on the Audiobooks playlist.

SETTING AUDIOBOOK PREFERENCES ON AN iPOD
You can control audiobook playback speed on the iPod.

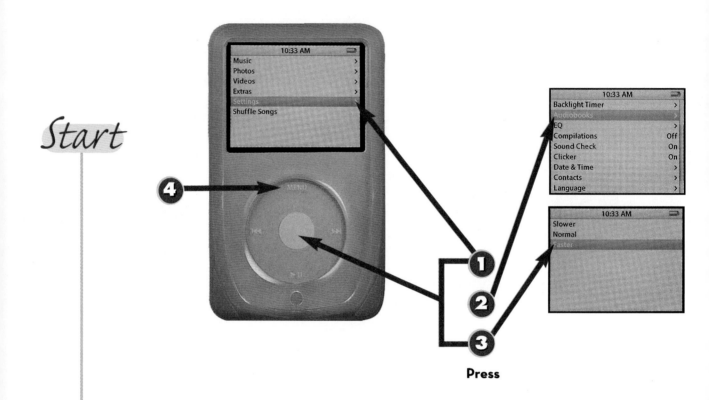

Start

Press

End

1. Choose **Settings** from the iPod's main menu and press the **center button**.

2. Choose **Audiobooks** from the Settings menu and press the **center button**.

3. Choose an audiobook speed option. All books are played back at the speed you've chosen.

4. Press **Menu** to exit the Audiobooks setting menu.

TIP
Safe at Any Speed
If you're not sure which speed will be most comfortable for you, try listening to a bit of an audiobook using each of the three settings.

NOTE
Kick It up a Notch
For some added physical protection from dings and scratches (not to mention a cool lookin' iPod) check out www.iskin.com for skins such as the evo3 seen here.

LISTENING TO AUDIOBOOKS ON AN iPOD

Audiobooks have their own playlist on your iPod. You can start and stop audiobook play-back without losing your place between listenings.

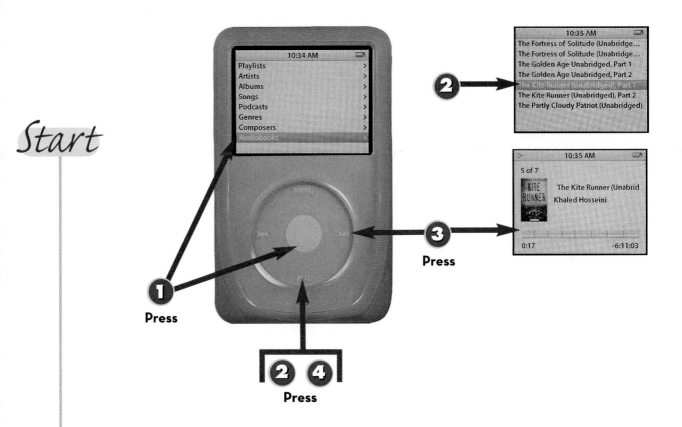

Start

Press

Press

Press

1 Choose **Audiobooks** from the iPod's Music menu and press the **center button**.

2 Scroll to the book you want to hear, and press **Play**.

3 If the book has been divided into chapters (you will see hash marks on the Status bar), press the **Next** button to move to the next chapter.

4 Press **Play/Stop** again to pause playback.

End

VIEWING PHOTOS ON AN iPOD

There's no need to carry photos in your wallet or lug around a photo album to show off to friends and family. With an iPod or iPod nano, you can display photos and play slideshows anytime, anywhere. You can also sync specific folders of photos or your iPhoto (Mac) library with your iPod, making it easy to keep a group of photos up-to-date.

With photos on your iPod, you can create slideshows—complete with music and transitions—or display groups of photos together. Using Apple's iPod AV cable, you can display your photos on a television.

To get photos onto your iPod, you sync a folder on your computer with the device, using iTunes. You can also use a camera adapter (from Apple or Belkin) to copy photos directly from a digital camera to your iPod or iPod nano.

VIEW PHOTOS ON YOUR iPOD

FINDING PHOTOS ON YOUR COMPUTER

Macs and PCs each have standard locations for photos. On a Mac, it's the Pictures folder in your home folder. Windows users store photos in My Pictures, inside the My Documents folder. You might have photos stored elsewhere. Before you import photos into an iPod, identify the folder that contains all the images you want to import, or choose a new one, as described in Part 12, "Using Your iPod As a PDA or Hard Drive," of this book.

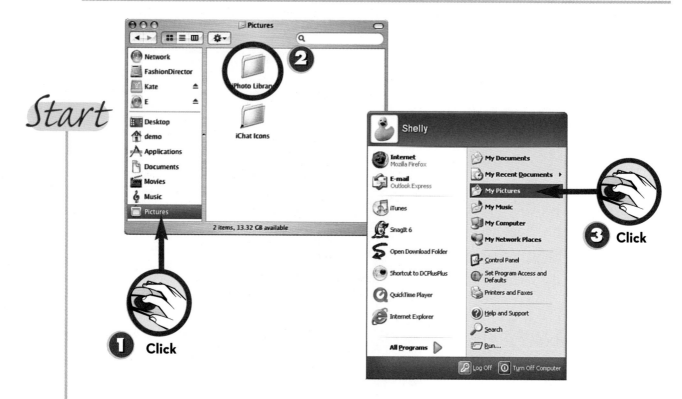

Start

1 Click

3 Click

End

1 (Mac) In the Finder, click the **Pictures** folder in the sidebar to see the contents of your Pictures folder.

2 (Mac) If you use Apple's iPhoto software, the Pictures folder contains a folder called iPhoto Library. You can sync your iPod with the library or a specific iPhoto album.

3 (Windows) Click the **Start** menu and choose **My Pictures** to see the contents of your photo folder.

TIP
Sync Other Folders
You can sync a folder other than the standard My Pictures or Pictures folder, but you first need to add the photos you want to include on your iPod by dragging and dropping the pictures into the desired folder.

NOTE
Nested Folders
Subfolders are also available for syncing to your iPod. You can sync to either the entire folder you select or several of its subfolders. Using subfolders, you can create photo playlists to organize iPod photos and to play slideshows.

SETTING PHOTO SYNCING PREFERENCES IN iTUNES

Although iTunes does not store or manage your photos, you must use it to set up and sync photos from your computer to your iPod.

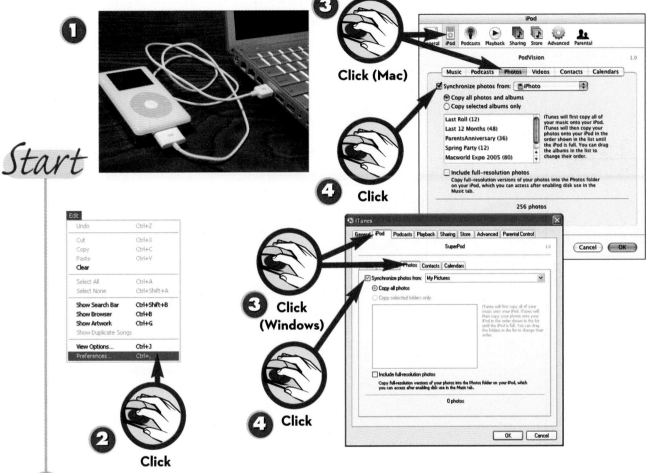

Click (Mac)

Click

Click (Windows)

Click

Click

Start

End

1. Connect a photo-capable iPod to your computer.

2. In iTunes, choose **iTunes**, **Preferences** (Mac) or **Edit**, **Preferences** (Windows).

3. Click **iPod** and then click the **Photos** tab.

4. To sync your default photo folder with the iPod, click the **Synchronize Photos From** check box. iTunes automatically selects iPhoto (Mac) or My Pictures (Windows).

SYNC ALBUMS FROM YOUR MAC'S iPHOTO LIBRARY

If you choose to sync a Mac's iPhoto library to your iPod, iTunes displays all of your iPhoto albums. You can choose to sync only specific albums if you want.

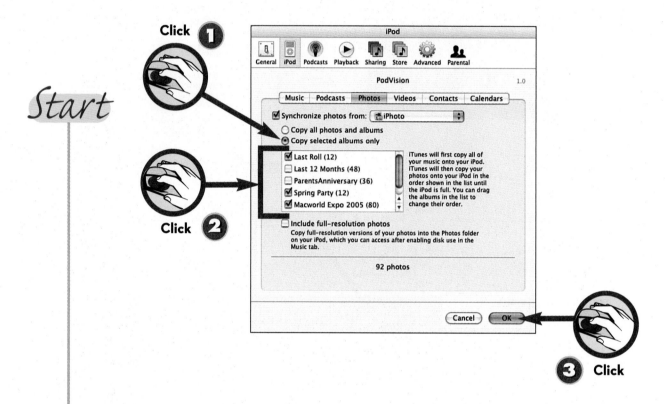

1. With iPhoto selected in iTunes's Photo syncing preferences area, click **Copy Selected Albums Only**.

2. Click check boxes next to the albums you want to sync with the iPod.

3. Click **OK**.

NOTE

Date-Based Albums

In addition to the iPhoto albums you create to keep your photo collection organized, iPhoto's date-based default albums appear when you choose to sync specific iPhoto albums. Because they're date-based, the contents of these iPhoto albums change over time. If you sync a date-based album, you always have your most recent photos on your iPod.

SYNC PHOTOS AND FOLDERS FROM YOUR MY PICTURES FOLDER IN WINDOWS

Photos you've stored in My Pictures and in subfolders within My Pictures can be quickly synced to your iPod.

Start

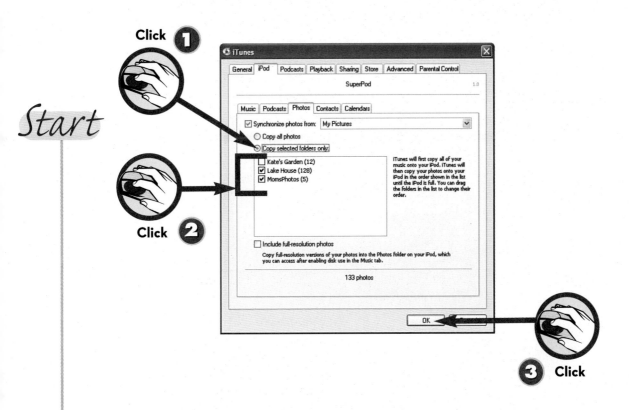

Click ① — ... ②

Click ③ **Click**

① With My Pictures selected in iTunes's Photo syncing preferences area, click **Copy Selected Folders Only**.

② Click check boxes next to the subfolders you want to sync with the iPod.

③ Click **OK**.

End

NOTE

Finding Folders

If you use an application that imports photos into your My Pictures folder, you see those pictures and any folders your application creates within it when you open iTunes's Photo preferences.

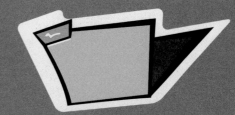

CHOOSE FOLDERS TO SYNC WITH YOUR iPOD

If you don't want to sync your default picture folder (Pictures on the Mac, My Pictures in Windows) with your iPod, you can create or choose a different folder—any folder on your computer.

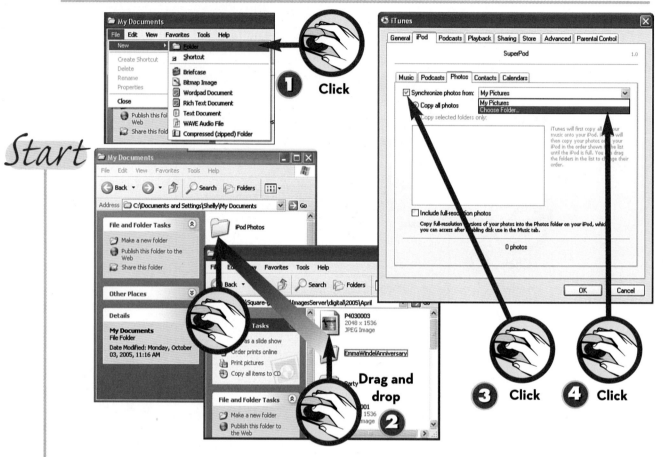

Start

Click

Drag and drop

3 Click   4 Click

1 In Windows Explorer, choose **File**, **New**, **Folder** to create a new folder for the photos you want to sync to your iPod.

2 Drag photos or folders containing photos into the new folder.

3 With an iPod connected to your computer, open **iTunes Preferences** and click **iPod** and then the **Photos** tab. Click the **Synchronize Photos From** check box.

4 Click the adjacent drop-down menu and select **Choose Folder**.

Continued

TIP

iPod Folder Benefits

Think of picture folders and subfolders synced to your iPod as photo playlists. On your iPod, a folder full of photos can be displayed as a slideshow on the iPod screen or on a television.

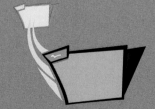

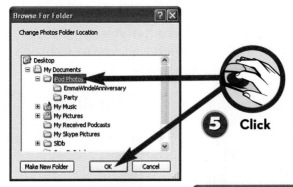

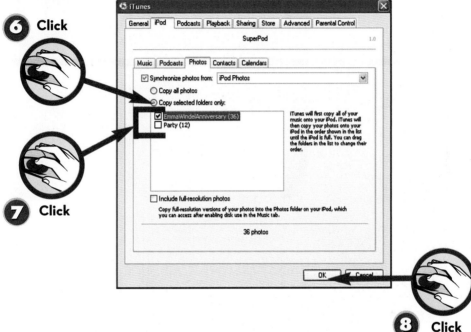

5 Navigate to the folder you want to sync and click **OK**. The folder's name appears in iTunes's preferences, along with any subfolders inside it.

6 To sync several subfolders within a folder you've selected, click the **Copy Selected Folders Only** radio button.

7 Click check boxes for each folder you want to add to the sync.

8 Click **OK** to close iTunes's preferences.

End

NOTE

Organize

Even if you don't use iPhoto or some other tool to organize the photos you store on your computer, having a photo-friendly iPod is a great excuse to organize your photos. Create a folder for all the photos you plan to sync to the iPod, plus subfolders to organize the photos by subject or date.

VIEWING PHOTOS ON YOUR iPOD

The iPod organizes photos based on the folders on your computer you have synced to it. If you sync your Mac's iPhoto library or My Pictures folder (Windows), you'll see playlists on the iPod for the Pictures folder and each album or folder within it.

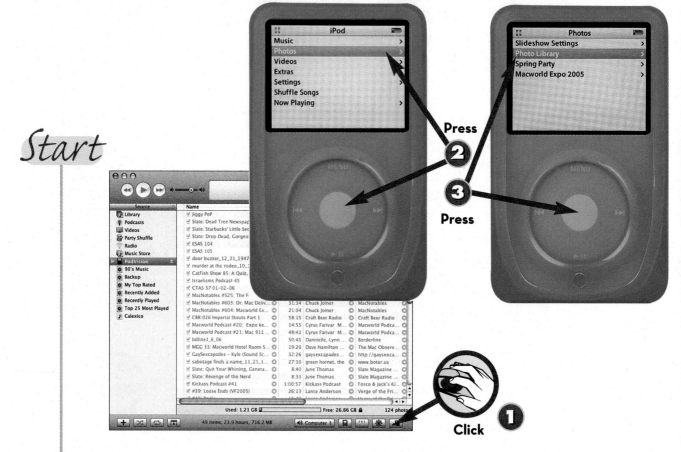

Start

Press

Press

Click

1. In iTunes, check the display to be sure the iPod is not being synced and click **Eject** to unmount the iPod.

2. Select **Photos** from the iPod's main menu and press the **center button**.

3. Select **Photo Library** and press the **center button**.

Continued

Press

Press

Press

4 Press the **Previous** or **Next** button to see another photo.

5 Press **Menu** to return to the thumbnail view.

6 Press **Menu** again to see the Photos menu. If you have added photo subfolders or albums from an iPhoto library, you see them on this menu.

End

TIP
Hi-Res Photos on Your iPod
iTunes copies low-resolution versions of your photos onto your iPod by default. This saves lots of disk space. If you want to store the original, higher-resolution versions of images on the iPod, enable the **Include Full-Resolution Photos** check box in iTunes preferences. After you enable disk use under the Music tab of iPod preferences, you are able to copy the hi-res photos from the iPod to your computer.

PLAYING A SLIDESHOW ON YOUR iPOD

Your iPod plays a slideshow including all of the images in an album or folder.

Start

①
Press

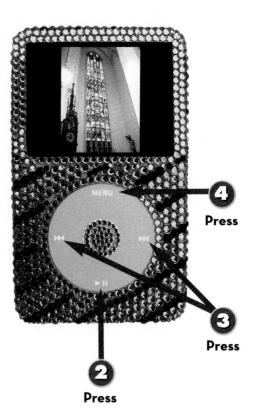

④
Press

③
Press

②
Press

① From the iPod's **Photos** menu, select a folder or Photo Library and press the **center button**.

② Press the **Play** button to see a slideshow. Press **Play** again to pause.

③ Press **Previous** or **Next** to go back or advance one slide.

④ Press **Menu** to end the slideshow.

End

NOTE

Add Some Bling

If you like the crystal-studded look that the iPod in this task has, check out
http://crystalicing.com for other design options. You can send in your iPod (or digital camera,
PDA, cell phone, and so on) and Crystal Icing's master artisans will turn it into a work of art.
You can also order do-it-yourself kits if you are artsy and want to try this yourself.

CHOOSING SLIDESHOW SETTINGS

You can choose music, transitions, and the slide duration for your iPod slideshow.

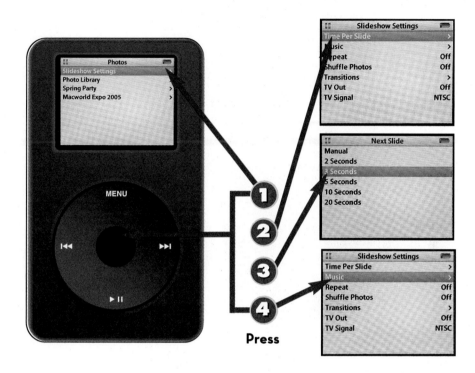

Start

Press

1 Select **Slideshow Settings** from the Photos menu and press the **center button**.

2 Select **Time Per Slide** and press the **center button**.

3 Choose an option from the menu. You are returned to the Slideshow Settings menu.

4 Select **Music** and press the **center button**. Choose a playlist to use with your slideshow. You don't have the option to choose individual songs.

Continued

NOTE

Pick Your Music

If you want to use a single song to go with your slideshow, create a playlist that contains only that song.

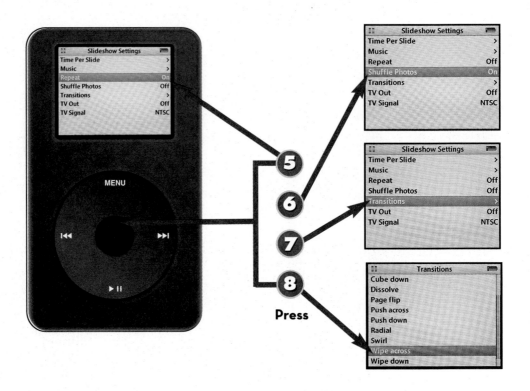

Press

⑤ Select **Repeat** and press the **center button** to toggle on or off the option.

⑥ Select **Shuffle Photos** and press the **center button** to choose On or Off.

⑦ Select **Transitions** and press the **center button**.

⑧ Choose an option from the list.

Continued

 TIP
Just the Right Tune
If you want your iPod to play a specific song rather than a playlist when you run a slideshow, create a playlist containing only the song or songs you want to use with the slideshow. Don't forget to sync the playlist to your iPod if you are not automatically syncing your entire library.

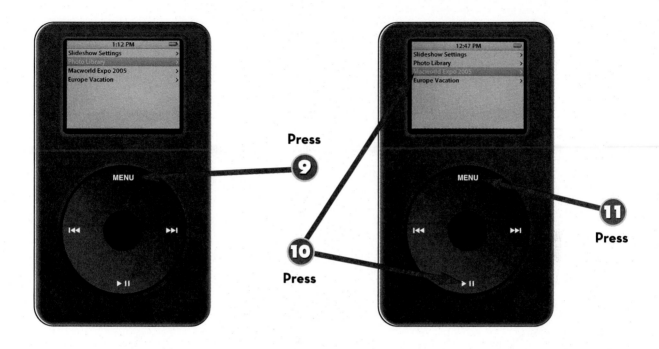

9 To view a sideshow with its new settings, press **Menu** to see the list of photo folders.

10 Select a folder and press **Play**.

11 Press **Menu** to end the slideshow.

End

TIP

Photos and Slideshows on TV

If you have an Apple iPod AV adapter, you can display photos or a slideshow on a television. Connect the adapter to your TV and iPod, as described in Part 9, "Watching Video in iTunes and on Your iPod," and use the **TV Out** and **TV Signal** options on the Slideshow Settings menu to get the signal onto your TV.

USING YOUR iPOD AS A PDA OR HARD DISK

The iPod's primary job is to play music, other audio programs, and video, but you can also use it to store your contacts and your schedule. You'll also find a few games on the iPod, for those long plane or train rides. The iPod can even serve as a portable hard disk, for those times when you need to move files between home and work or school. The iPod's PDA features are available on standard iPods and the iPod nano. You can use any iPod, including the shuffle, as a hard disk.

Like a PDA or cell phone, you can sync your computer's address book and calendar with an iPod. Unlike those other portable devices, you can't make changes to your contacts on an iPod. It's easiest to sync contacts and calendars if you use Address Book and iCal on the Mac, or a version of Microsoft Outlook on a Windows computer. You can, however, add information from other contact management software—it just takes a few extra steps.

iPod games range from Breakout to Solitaire to a music quiz featuring your library of songs. In this part you'll also learn how to add games and text-based reference information. You can use your iPod as a stopwatch or an alarm clock, too, and create clocks for time zones around the world for quick reference while you travel.

iPOD EXTRAS

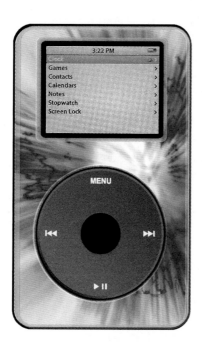

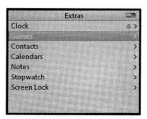

AUTOMATICALLY SYNCING MAC CONTACTS AND CALENDARS WITH YOUR iPOD

To automatically add contacts and calendar information to your iPod, you must use **Address Book** to manage your contacts and **iCal** to manage calendar events and to-do items. From there, you copy contact data to your iPod using iTunes.

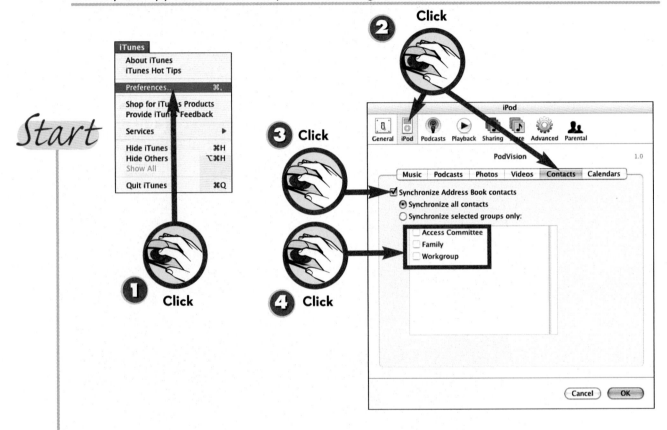

Start

Click (2)

Click (3)

Click (1)

Click (4)

1. With your iPod connected to your computer, open iTunes and choose **iTunes, Preferences**.

2. Click **iPod**, and then the **Contacts** tab.

3. Click to check the **Synchronize Address Book Contents** check box. By default, all contacts are added to your iPod.

4. To sync only contacts that are part of an Address Book group, click **Synchronize Selected Groups Only** and click the check boxes of the groups you want to include.

Continued

TIP
Creating Groups
To create groups you can use to synchronize selected contacts with your iPod, open Address Book and click the **Plus** button. Name the group and add contacts by dragging them from the middle pane of Address Book.

TIP
Photos from Address Book
The Address Book contact manager supports associating a photo to each contact. Just drag an image onto the image box. Syncing a contact with a photo adds the photo to your iPod.

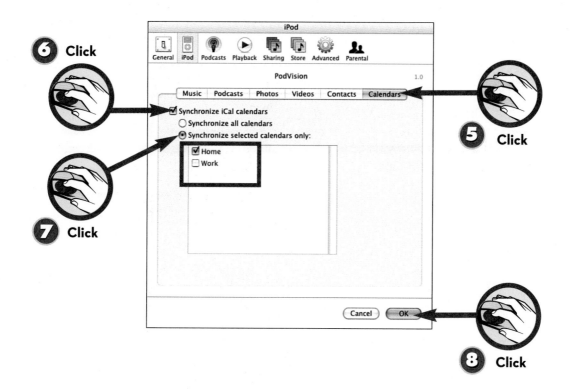

6 Click

7 Click

5 Click

8 Click

5 Click the **Calendars** tab.

6 Click to check the **Synchronize iCal Calendars** check box.

7 To synchronize only certain calendars, click **Synchronize Selected Calendars Only**. Click check boxes for each calendar you want to add to the iPod.

8 Click **OK**.

End

TIP
iCal Calendars
By default, iCal includes calendars called Home and Work. To add a new one, choose **File**, **New Calendar in iCal**. When you add a new iCal event, assign it to a calendar by choosing the calendar in the iCal info pane.

TIP
Syncing with Older Versions of Mac OS X
Mac OS X versions prior to 10.4 (Tiger) do not support contact syncing in iTunes. You can, however, use Apple's iSync application (included with Mac OS X) to do the job.

AUTOMATICALLY SYNCING WINDOWS CONTACTS AND CALENDARS WITH YOUR iPOD

To automatically add contacts from a Windows computer to your iPod, you must be using Microsoft Outlook or Outlook Express to manage them. To add calendars, you need Outlook.

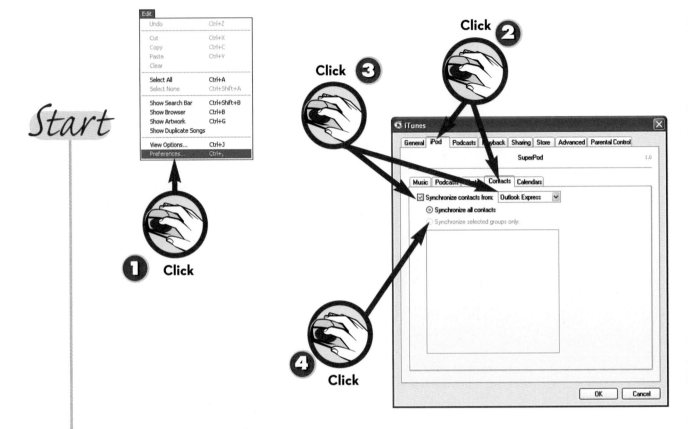

1 With your iPod connected to your computer, open iTunes and choose **Edit**, **Preferences**.

2 Click **iPod** and then the **Contacts** tab.

3 Click the **Synchronize Contacts From** check box, and choose **Outlook** or **Outlook Express** from the drop-down menu.

4 If you are using Outlook groups and want to sync selected contacts, click the **Synchronize Selected Groups Only** radio button and then check boxes for groups you want to include.

Continued

TIP

Better Outlook Syncing

The iPod's built-in contact syncing features are okay, but you can get more information out of Outlook and Outlook Express with iPodSoft's PodPlus ($12, www.ipodsoft.com). With PodPlus installed, iTunes gives you more syncing options: Outlook email, notes, and tasks. You can also sync RSS-based weather, horoscopes, and movie listings. They appear as notes on your iPod.

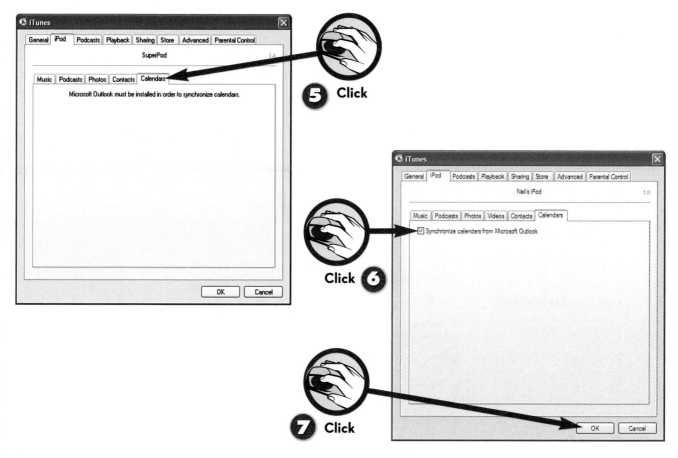

5 Click the **Calendars** tab. You are able to sync calendars only if Microsoft Outlook is installed on your computer.

6 Click the **Synchronize Calendars from Microsoft Outlook** check box.

7 Click **OK**.

End

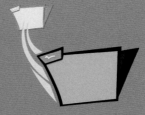

MANUALLY SYNCING CONTACTS AND CALENDARS

If you don't use Apple or Microsoft contact management software (or even if you do), you can manually add contacts to your iPod by dragging files from your computer to the iPod. First, you need to enable disk use on the iPod.

Click (Mac)

Click (Windows)

Click

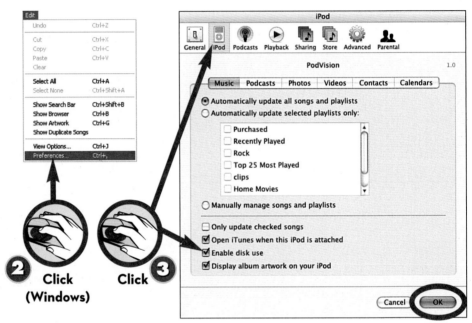

1 Connect an iPod to your computer.

2 If disk use is not already enabled for this iPod, open iTunes and then click **iTunes**, **Preferences** (Mac), or **Edit**, **Preferences** (Windows).

3 Click **iPod** and then click **Enable Disk Use**. Click **OK** to close iTunes Preferences.

Continued

TIP

If Dragging Doesn't Work
You can drag contacts from popular email programs including Palm Desktop, Eudora, and Microsoft Entourage. If you use another program to manage your contacts and find that dragging does not work, first export contacts from your email program or contact manager and then drag the resulting file into the iPod's Contacts folder.

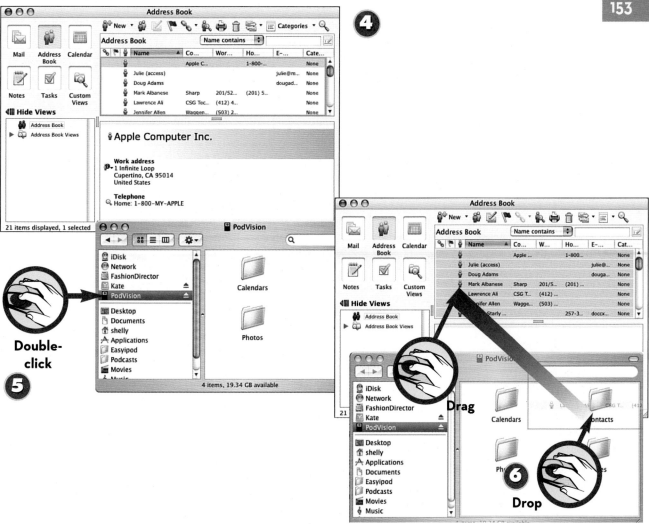

Double-click

5

Drag

Drop

6

4 Open your email program and view the address book.

5 Locate your iPod in the Mac Finder or using Windows Explorer. Double-click the **iPod** icon to open it.

6 Drag contacts from the application's address book to the iPod's **Contacts** folder.

Continued

NOTE
No Manual To-Dos

iCal files you export and add to your iPod manually do not include to-do items. You can only add to-do items by syncing iCal or Outlook with the iPod.

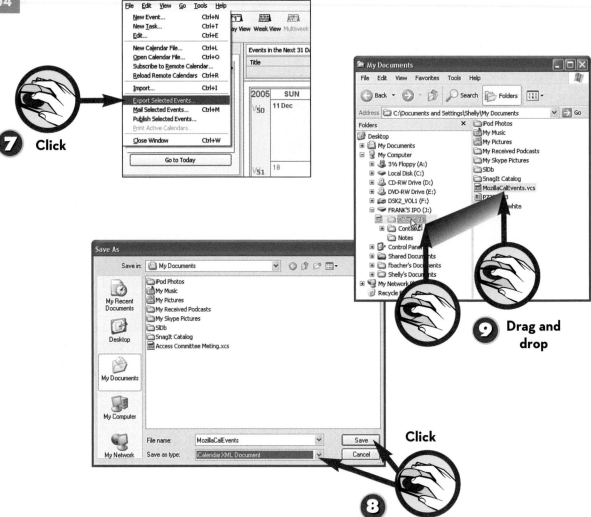

7 Click

8

9 Drag and drop

Click

7 Open your calendar application and export calendar events in the iCalendar format by choosing **File**, **Export Selected Events**. (Depending on your calendar application, this option might be named something slightly different.)

8 Name the file, choose an iCalendar export option, and click **Save**.

9 Drag the resulting **.ics** (Mac) or **.vcs** (Windows) file into the iPod's **Calendars** folder.

End

NOTE

Other Ways To Sync

Several iPod utilities are available to help you sync calendar information with an iPod. They include iPodSync ($15, www.ipod-sync.com) for Windows and Pod2Go ($12, www.kainjow.com/pod2go).

ADDING NOTES TO AN iPOD

You can copy text files to your iPod for reference on the go. Unlike calendars and contacts, the default way to add notes is to drag files onto your iPod, rather than using iTunes. You must enable disk access to the iPod to add notes (see step 2 in this task). You also can use shareware tools to automatically add notes.

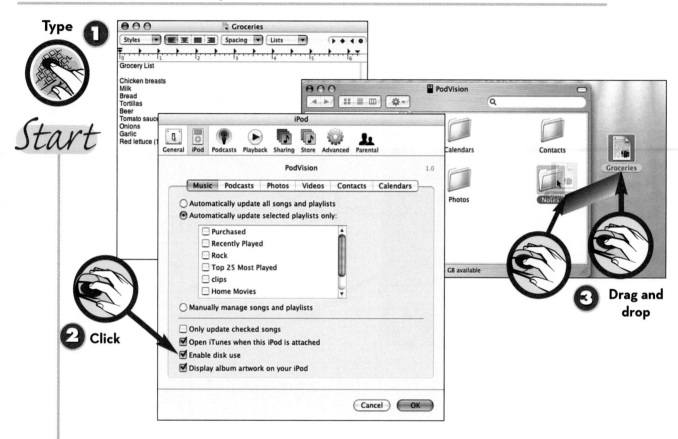

Type ❶

Start

2 Click

3 Drag and drop

End

❶ Create and save a text file on your computer. WordPad (Windows) or TextEdit (Mac) create plain text files, as do many other applications.

❷ Connect an iPod to your computer. If the iPod is not already enabled for disk use, open the iTunes Preferences dialog box and click **Enable Disk Use** in the iPod's **Music** tab.

❸ In the Finder (Mac) or Windows Explorer (Windows), drag the text file you created into the iPod's **Notes** folder.

NOTE

Notes Managers

Pod2Go can also manage notes for iPod Mac users, even downloading news, stock quotes, movie listings, and other information that can be turned into iPod notes. Anapod Explorer for Windows ($25, www.redchairsoftware.com/anapod) also manages notes.

VIEWING CONTACTS ON AN iPOD

Mac users will immediately recognize the Contacts screen on the iPod. It looks much like the Address Book application's interface. Windows users get the same information, minus the photo.

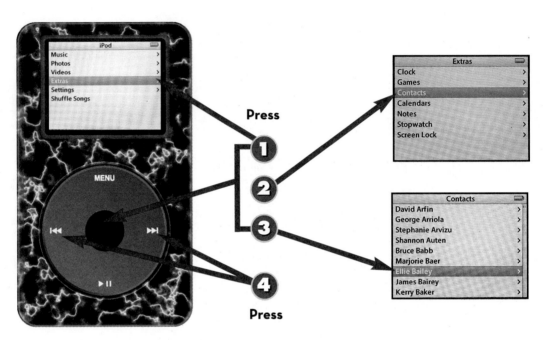

Press

Press

1 From the iPod main menu, scroll to **Extras** and press the **center button** to select it.

2 Select **Contacts** and press the **center button**. A list of contacts appears.

3 Choose a contact and press the **center button** to see its details.

4 Use the **Previous** and **Next** buttons to move among contacts.

NOTE
If you like the look of the skin seen in these examples, check out www.designerskins.com for more cool way to express yourself with your iPod.

SETTING iPOD CONTACT OPTIONS

You can tell the iPod how to sort and display your contacts. You can choose from two options for both sorting and displaying.

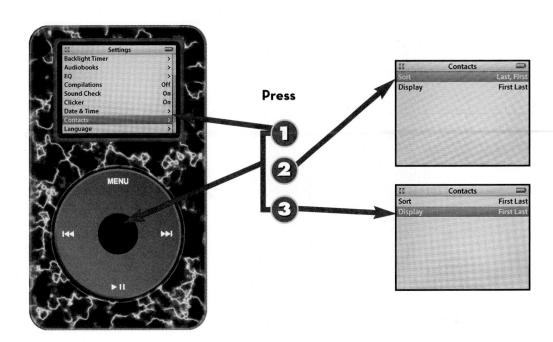

Start

Press

End

① From the iPod's main menu, choose **Settings**, **Contacts**.

② Toggle the **Sort** menu to sort contacts by first, last name or last, first name.

③ Toggle the **Display** menu to view contacts by first, last name or last, first name.

VIEWING CALENDAR EVENTS ON AN iPOD

If you have created multiple calendars (work, school, and home, for example) in iCal or Outlook, you can view them together or separately on your iPod.

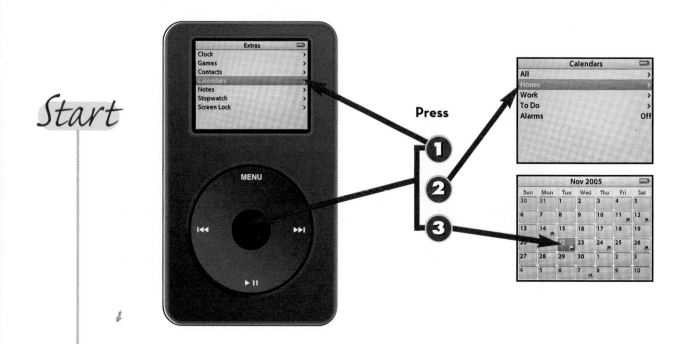

Press

Start

1 Choose **Extras**, **Calendars** and press the **center button**.

2 Select from the list of calendars to see the current month's events and press the **center button**. To see events from all calendars, choose **All**.

3 Use the click wheel to move to a day whose events you want to see, and press the **center button**.

Continued

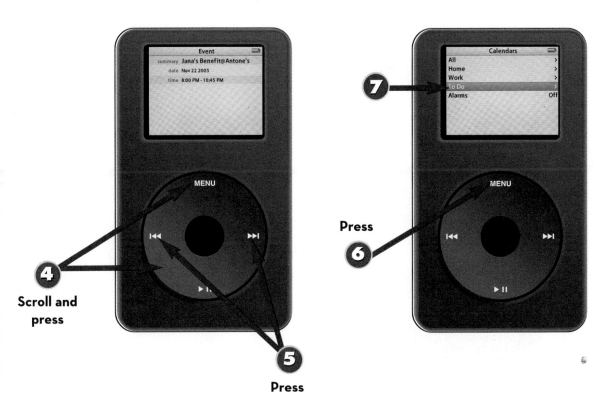

4 Scroll to see all events and their descriptions. Press **Menu** to return to the calendar.

5 Press the **Previous** or **Next** button to move between months.

6 To view to-do items (you must have imported iCal or Outlook to-do items automatically), press the **Menu** button to return to the Calendars menu.

7 Choose **To Do** and press the **center button** to see the list.

End

VIEWING NOTES ON AN iPOD

Text files you have added to your iPod appear as notes.

Start

Press

Press

Scroll

1 Select **Extras**, **Notes** and press the **center button**.

2 Select a note and press the **center button**.

3 Scroll through the note to read it.

4 Press **Menu** to return to the list of notes.

End

PLAYING GAMES ON AN iPOD

The iPod and iPod nano include several games: tiny arcade-style offerings, solitaire, and a version of Name That Tune, with your music library as the star.

Start

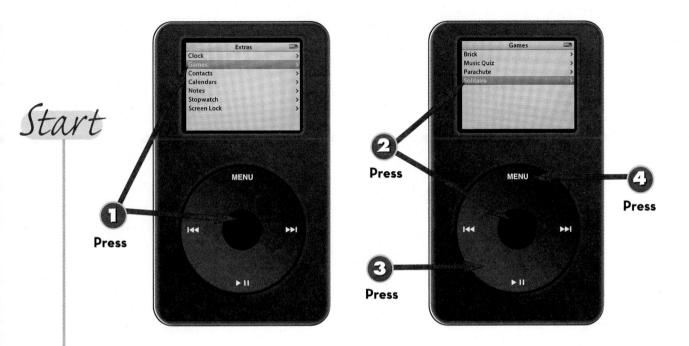

1 Press

2 Press

3 Press

4 Press

1 Choose **Extras**, **Games**.

2 Select a game from the list and press the **center button** to begin playing.

3 Use the iPod's **Play**, **Previous**, **Next** and **center button** to navigate within the game.

4 Press **Menu** to end the game.

End

ADDING GAMES AND TEXT-BASED APPLICATIONS TO YOUR iPOD

You can buy text-based adventure and trivia games for your iPod. Other text-based iPod tools include recipe collections and event schedules.

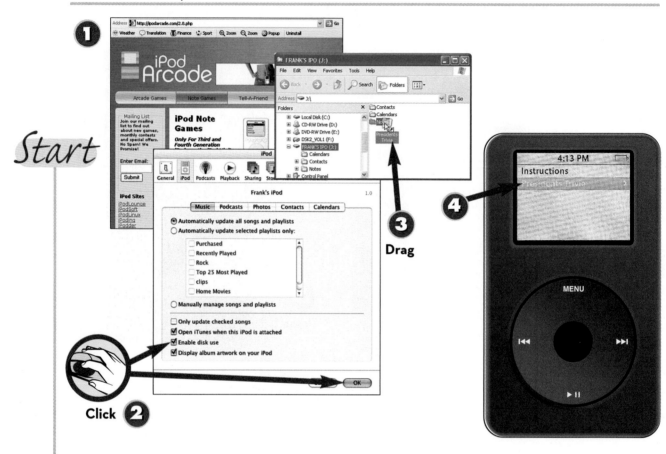

Start

Click **2**

3 Drag

4

1 Download and unzip an iPod game.

2 Connect an iPod to your computer, being sure that disk use is enabled in iTunes iPod music preferences (**Edit**, **Preferences** [Windows] or **iTunes**, **Preferences** [Mac]).

3 In the Finder (Mac) or Windows Explorer (Windows), drag the game folder into the iPod's **Notes** folder.

4 Disconnect the iPod and look for your new game on the **Notes** menu.

End

TIP
Sources of iPod Games
A number of companies offer iPod games, including Malinche (www.malinche.net/); XOPlay (www.xoplay.com); and iPod Arcade (www.ipodarcade.com), whose offerings are all free.

TIP
Sources of iPod Information
Kraft Foods (www.kraftfoods.com/kf/ff/ipod/ipod.html) offers a recipe collection. PartyPod Pro ($9.50, www.helmesinnovations.com/PartyPodPro.html) includes drink recipes and more. CitizenPod (http://citizenpod.com) has music festival listings.

CREATING iPOD CLOCKS

As you learned back in Part 2, "Connecting Your iPod to a Mac or PC," you can set your iPod's date and time. Clocks allow you to save information for several time zones so you can quickly call up the correct time all around the world.

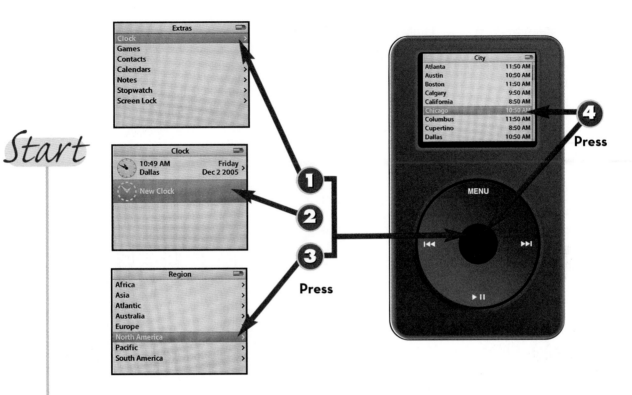

Start

Press

Press

1 Choose **Extras**, **Clock**.

2 Select **New Clock** and press the **center button**.

3 Choose a continent and press the **center button**.

4 Choose a city or country and press the **center button** to finish creating the clock.

End

TIP

Too Many Clocks?

Clocks are a cool iPod feature, but too many might slow the iPod's performance or run down the battery. It's a good idea to delete clocks you don't need to keep your iPod running in top form.

USING AN iPOD AS A HARD DISK

Using an iPod to store files, just like a hard disk, is as simple as enabling disk use in iTunes Preferences. You must do this on an iPod or iPod nano when the iPod is set to sync automatically. If you manually update your iPod, you don't need to enable disk use.

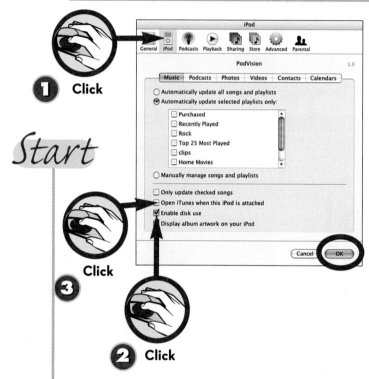

Start

1 Click

3 Click

2 Click

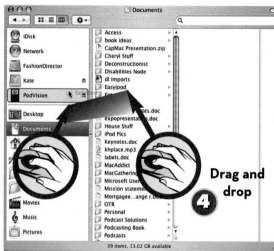

4 Drag and drop

1 With an automatically synced iPod connected, select **Edit**, **Preferences** (Windows) or **iTunes**, **Preferences** (Mac) to open iTunes Preferences. Click the **iPod** button.

2 Click the **Enable Disk Use** check box.

3 If you intend to access the iPod hard disk frequently, you might want to uncheck the **Open iTunes When This iPod Is Attached** check box to save time. Click **OK**.

4 To store files on your iPod, drag them from the Finder (Mac) or Window Explorer (Windows) to the iPod item.

End

TIP

One iPod, One Computer

Your iPod is formatted for the kind of computer you first used with it: Mac or Windows PC. You can't use the files you've stored on a Mac-formatted iPod with a Windows computer, and vice versa.

USING AN iPOD SHUFFLE AS A HARD DISK

You can use an iPod shuffle (limited though its space might be) as a hard disk, too. The options are a bit different.

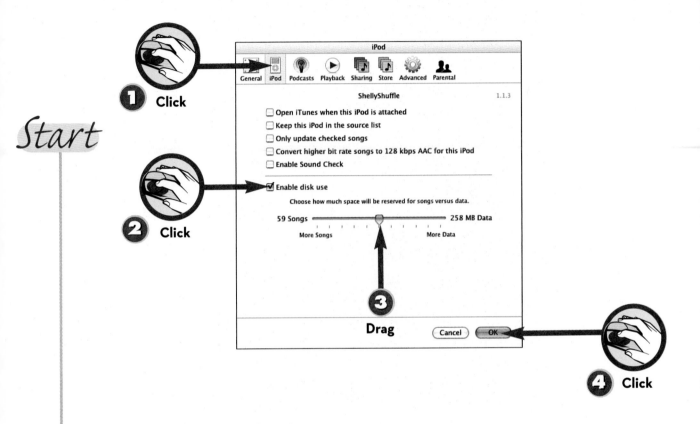

Start

① **Click**

② **Click**

③ **Drag**

④ **Click**

① With an iPod shuffle connected to your computer, open iTunes Preferences and click the **iPod** button.

② Click the **Enable Disk Use** check box.

③ Drag the slider to reserve more or less space for file storage. The space you reserve becomes unavailable for music.

④ Click **OK**.

End

TIP

Shuffle Owner's Prerogative

Even after you have chosen an amount of space you want to devote to data storage, you can change your mind later by adjusting the Disk Use slider in iTunes's iPod shuffle preferences.

NOTE

Shuffle Speaks Two Languages

Unlike its larger cousins, the iPod shuffle can be used as a hard disk for both a Mac and a Windows PC. Larger iPods must be linked to one type of computer, and must be reformatted to work with the other type.

MANAGING YOUR iTUNES LIBRARY

Like house plants and long-term relationships, your iTunes library requires care and feeding. You can move, delete, and edit the library's contents when things become cluttered, or simply to make it easier to find things.

iTunes's powerful ID3 tag editing tools enable you to fix mistakes that came into your library along with songs you've ripped or purchased. You can even edit groups of files to associate them with one another.

Music ratings in iTunes and on the iPod help you find and play the music you want to hear. Party Shuffle and iTunes smart playlists work with ratings to bring the best songs to the forefront.

Deleting songs or song references in your iTunes library helps cut down on clutter or broken links, as does iTunes's Show Duplicate Songs feature.

EDIT ID3 TAGS

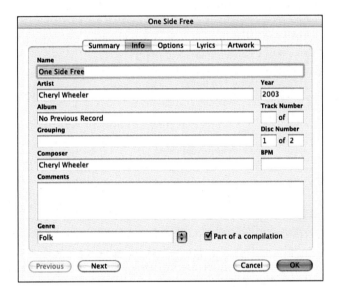

EDITING SONG INFO IN iTUNES

The name, artist, album, and other information about every track in your iTunes music library is stored in ID3 tags. You can edit ID3 tags to correct errors or add missing information.

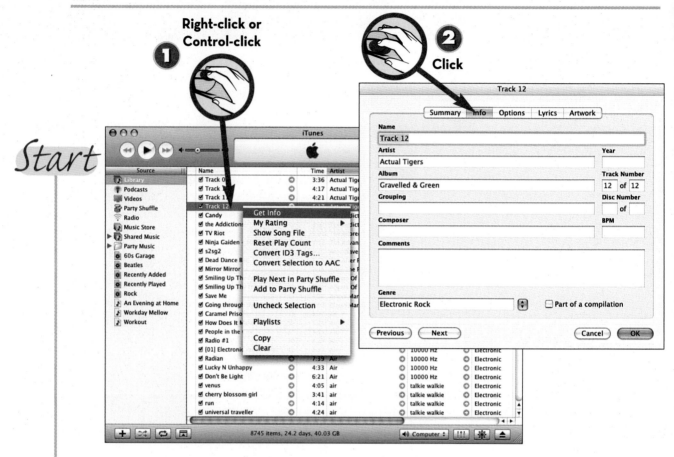

Right-click or Control-click

1

2

Click

Start

1 In iTunes, select a song, podcast, or audiobook file, and right-click (Windows) or Control-click (Mac) and choose **Get Info**.

2 Click the **Info** tab.

Continued

NOTE

Why Edit?

If every bit of information supplied by Gracenote was accurate, and if every podcaster created ID3 tags for his show, you wouldn't need to edit ID3 tags. Besides misspellings in databases or empty tags, you can enhance a file's ID3 tags by changing or adding a genre that you can use to create smart playlists.

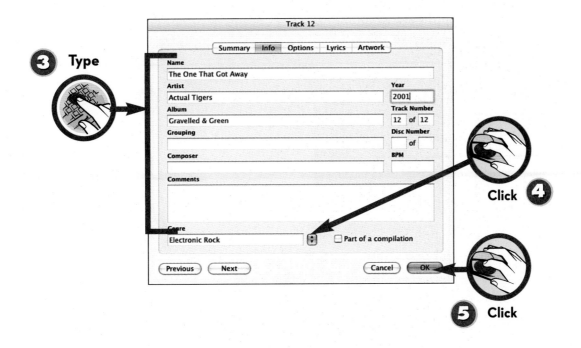

3 Type

Click **4**

5 Click

3 Edit the **Name**, **Artist**, **Album**, or one of the other fields.

4 To change the item's genre, click the menu next to the **Genre** field. If no genre is listed, type the first letter of the genre you want to use. iTunes fills in the rest. Keep typing if the first choice isn't the one you want.

5 Click **OK** when you are finished editing this song's ID3 tags.

End

—TIP—
Convert ID3 Tags

Songs that were ripped to a computer using a program other than iTunes (and sometimes even audio CDs you convert your-self) often have Artist and Song tags reversed. You can sometimes fix this with the Convert ID3 Tags command. Select a song and choose **Advanced**, **Convert ID3 Tags**. Choose a version from the drop-down menu (use trial and error because there's no way to tell which tag version was used), and then click **OK** to see if the tags have been corrected.

EDITING MULTIPLE ITEMS

You can edit tags for several songs at once. Do this to ensure that all items in a group have exactly the same tags. You can also use this command to make global changes to the sound or rating of all selected items.

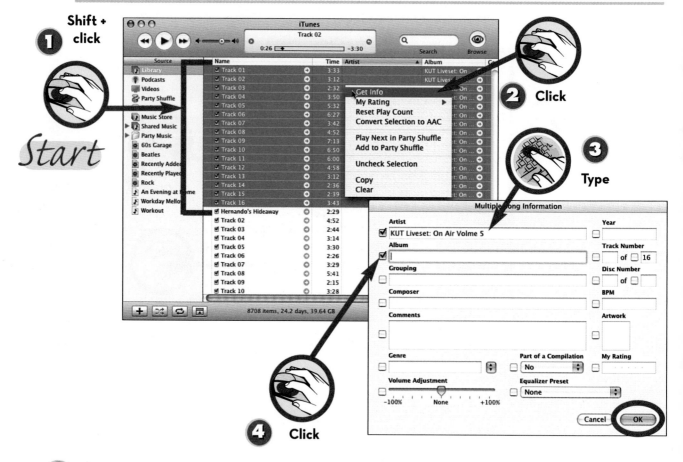

Shift + click 1

Start

2 **Click**

3 **Type**

4 **Click**

1 Select several items that should share an ID3 tag, such as an **Artist** or **Album**.

2 Control-click (Mac) or right-click (Windows) and choose **Get Info**. Click **OK** when iTunes asks if you're sure you want to edit multiple items.

3 Type the tag you want the selected items to share. Leave the other tags unchanged.

4 If you click the check box next to a blank field, this tag will be blank in all of the selected items. Click **OK**.

End

TIP

Multiple Blanks

In some cases, you might want all selected files to share the same tag—a blank one. Perhaps you want to make global changes to the Artist tag, but save updates to the Composer or Album tag for later. With multiple items selected and the Info window visible, click the check box next to a tag you want to leave blank. Delete any text currently in the field. When you click **OK**, iTunes makes tags for the selected items blank.

RATING YOUR MUSIC IN iTUNES

Rating your music is a great way to be sure that you hear the songs you like best more often. You can use music ratings to build smart playlists, to control which items are synced to your iPod, and to improve the Party Shuffle playlist.

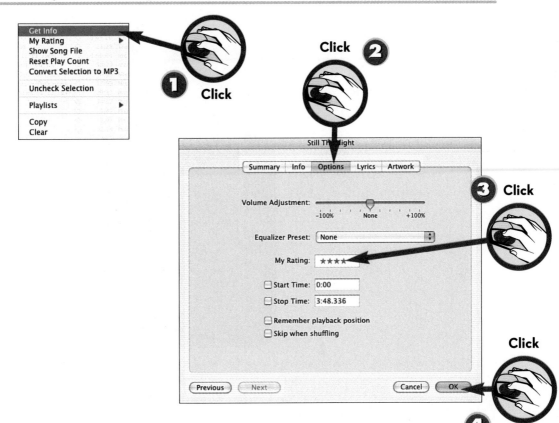

Start

End

1. Right-click (Windows) or Control-click (Mac) a song in iTunes and choose **Get Info** to open the Info window.

2. Click the **Options** tab.

3. Click a dot in the **My Rating** field corresponding with the number of stars this track should have.

4. Click **OK** to close the Info window.

TIP

Quick Ratings

To rate a selected song quickly, Control-click (Mac) or right-click (Windows) and choose **My Rating** from the drop-down menu. From here, you can choose a rating from one to five stars.

NOTE

Bulk Ratings

Like other fields in the Info window, you can edit ratings for multiple files by selecting them all and applying a rating in the Options area.

RATING MUSIC ON AN iPOD

You can rate songs as they play on your iPod.

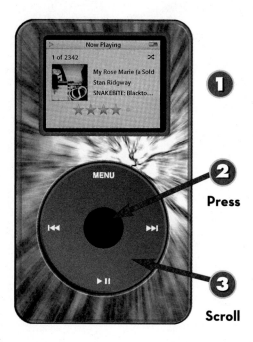

Start

End

① Begin playing a song on the iPod.

② Press the **center button** three times to reach the rating screen.

③ Use the click wheel to select a rating.

 NOTE

No Ratings for Podcasts on an iPod

You can't use an iPod to rate podcasts you download from iTunes, although you can rate them in iTunes. As a very useful consolation prize, press the **center button** three times while a podcast is playing. If the producer has included show notes, you see them on the screen.

DELETING DUPLICATE SONGS FROM YOUR LIBRARY

Deleting a song from your iTunes library removes both the music file and the item's listing in the iTunes library.

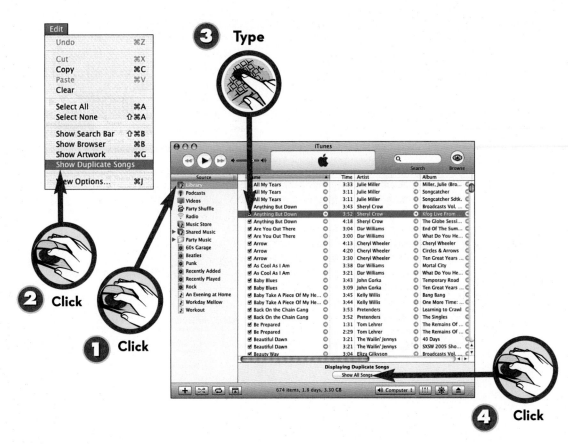

① Select the iTunes Library.

② Choose **Edit, Show Duplicate Songs**. iTunes displays files it thinks are duplicates. Some might be duplicate listings, while other might just be very similar to one another.

③ To remove one copy of a duplicate song, select it and press the **Delete** or **Backspace** key.

④ When you are finished pruning duplicates, click **Show All Songs**.

End

TIP

Are They Really Duplicates?

If you're not sure whether two library items really are identical, there are several ways to check. First, compare all ID3 tags for the files. You might find that two versions of the same song by the same artist appear on different albums. If the songs are different lengths, you might have a studio and a live version of the same song. To see whether two identical library listings point to the same file in your music folder, open each file's Info window and note the path in the Where section of the Summary tab.

DELETING SONGS FROM PLAYLISTS

There are three delete options in iTunes: remove a song listing from a specific playlist, remove a song listing from the music library, and remove a song file from your music library. You can also delete playlists without disturbing the files they reference.

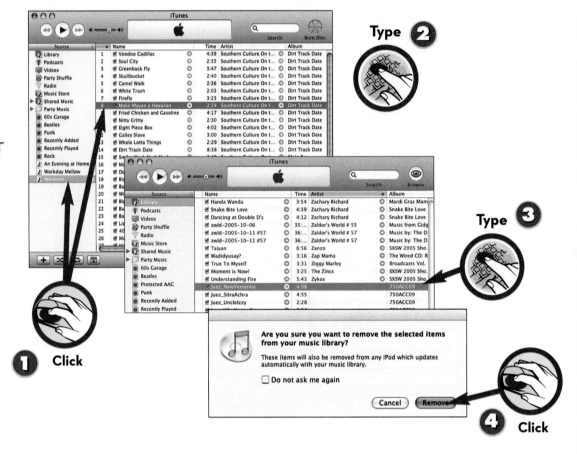

Type **2**

Type **3**

1 Click

4 Click

1 In iTunes, click a playlist and select a song you want to remove from the playlist.

2 Press the **Delete** or **Backspace** key. The song disappears from the playlist. The file is not deleted from the music library or your hard drive.

3 To delete a song listing from the music library, select **Library** and then select the song. Press the **Delete** or **Backspace** key.

4 The iTunes confirmation dialog opens and reminds you that the song will be deleted from your iPod the next time you sync it. Click **Remove**.

Continued

TIP
Which Playlist?
Before you delete a song from a specific playlist, you might want to see which (if any) other playlists include the song. With the song selected, Control-click (Mac) or right-click (Windows) and choose **Playlists** from the menu. You see them listed on a submenu.

NOTE
Uncheck, Don't Delete
To temporarily disable playback of a song without deleting it, uncheck it in iTunes. When you want to hear the song again, give its check box a click.

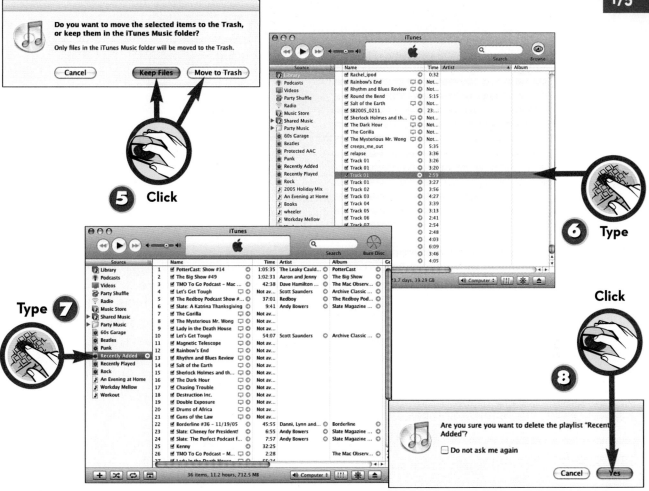

5 The next dialog box allows you to remove the song file from your hard disk. Click **Move to Trash** to delete the song, or **Keep Files** to do just that.

6 To delete a song from your computer (and your music library), press ⌘+**Delete** (Mac) or **Ctrl+Delete** (Windows).

7 To delete a playlist from iTunes, select it and press **Delete** or **Backspace**.

8 iTunes asks if you're sure you want to delete the playlist. Deleting a playlist does not affect the songs within it. Click **Yes**.

End

-TIP-
Not Smart
Because smart playlists consist of songs iTunes has found that match the criteria you set, you can't ordinarily delete a song from a smart playlist unless you delete it from the music library. The exception occurs if you have not enabled live updating when you created or edited the smart playlist. In that case, you can usually delete the item.

ADDING LYRICS AND ARTWORK TO YOUR MUSIC LIBRARY

iTunes and the iPod are about audio and video files. You can, however, add song lyrics, album art, and PDF files to the library to make your audio/video experience even cooler.

iTunes supports adding lyrics to any track in your music library. Songs don't come with lyrics, but you can use free or shareware software to search for, download, and add lyrics to iTunes and iPods that support them. Fifth generation iPods and iPod nanos support lyrics, as do some older models. Lyrics you download travel with the song, so if you add a track to a different music library, lyrics come along for the ride. Lyric information comes from one of several lyric databases. Mac users can choose from Dashboard widgets, full-on iPod management software, or AppleScript lyric downloaders. Windows users have fewer choices, but you can bring lyrics into your Windows-based music library, and I'll show you how later in this part.

iTunes Music Store purchases and many podcasts include album art that is visible in both iTunes and on a color iPod. You can also add artwork to any iTunes track, either by manually dragging an image into the library or by using freeware or shareware tools to find and download art for the selected track.

Portable Document Format (PDF) files are another way to store information about songs, such as liner notes, lyrics, and other text-based material. You can add a PDF to your iTunes library, too.

TRICKED OUT TUNES

ADDING LYRICS TO iTUNES ON A MAC

You can add lyrics to iTunes song files by downloading lyrics from the Internet and using software to add them automatically to your iTunes library. Pod2Go ($12, www.kainjow.com) is used in this example, but several other tools can do the job, as well.%

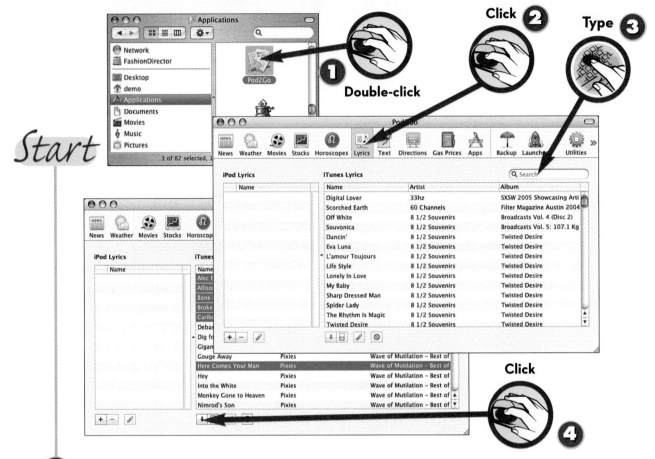

Start

1. In the **Applications** folder, double-click the **Pod2Go** icon.

2. Click the **Lyrics** button. Your music library's contents appear in the window.

3. In the **Search** field, type the artist, album, and/or song name for which you want to find lyrics.

4. From the search results, select the songs for which you want to download lyrics, and click the **Download** button.

Continued

TIP

Other Lyric Downloaders
Free or inexpensive Mac tools you can use to download lyrics to iTunes include KaraTunes ($11, http://ideographer.com/karatunes).

Click Start to download lyrics for the currently selected songs:

Cancel   Start

Click 5

Type 7   **Type** 6

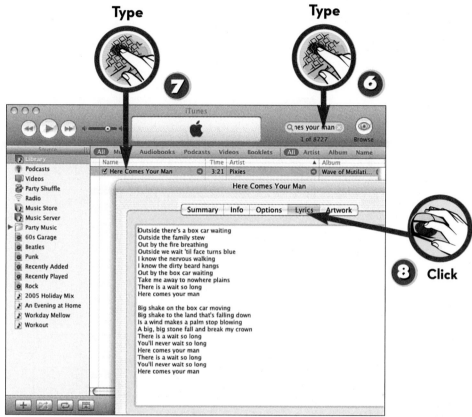

5 Click **Start** to begin the download. If Pod2Go cannot locate lyrics for a particular song, you see an error dialog listing the song.

6 Switch to iTunes and search for a song whose lyrics you have downloaded.

7 Select the song and press ⌘+I.

8 Click the **Lyrics** tab to see the downloaded lyrics.

End

TIP
You Too Can Be a Lyric Geek
Don't simply assume that the lyrics you download are accurate, or even that they're for the song you've selected. Many songs have similar titles, and lyrics in many databases come from fans, not from artists or record companies. Open a song's **Get Info** window in iTunes and check out the lyrics you've downloaded. You might even want to play the song while you read the lyrics.

ADDING LYRICS TO iTUNES ON A WINDOWS COMPUTER

Windows users have fewer options for downloading lyrics. One popular choice is iArt, which sets you back $10. Download it from www.ipodsoft.com. Besides downloading lyrics, iArt can fetch album art for your music. It is used again later in this part.

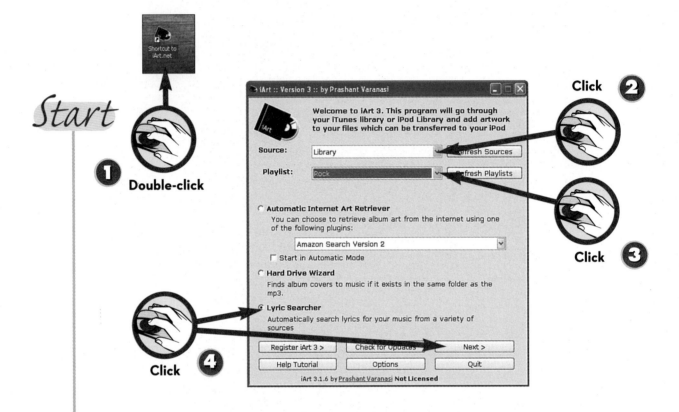

1. Double-click the shortcut on your desktop to launch **iArt**.

2. Choose a source from the **Source** drop-down menu. Sources can be your music library or an iPod.

3. Choose a standard playlist to scan. You can use the iTunes library, but a single playlist takes much less time if your library is large.

4. Click the **Lyric Searcher** radio button and then click **Next**.

Continued

 CAUTION

Beware Spyware

Before downloading lyric information or anything else from the Internet, be sure your system is protected from spyware and viruses. Tools such as Spyware Doctor ($29.95, www.pctools.com) and SpywareBlaster (free, www.javacoolsoftware.com) can locate and remove spyware and inoculate your machine against infections before they happen.

5 Click

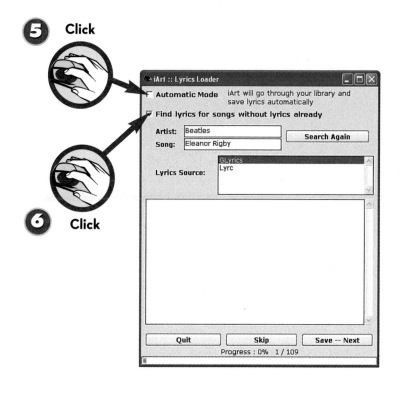

6 Click

5 Choose **Automatic Mode** to have iArt find lyrics for all songs in the selected playlist. Leave it unchecked to go through the list one song at a time.

6 To limit your search to songs without lyrics, click **Find Lyrics for Songs Without Lyrics Already**.

Continued

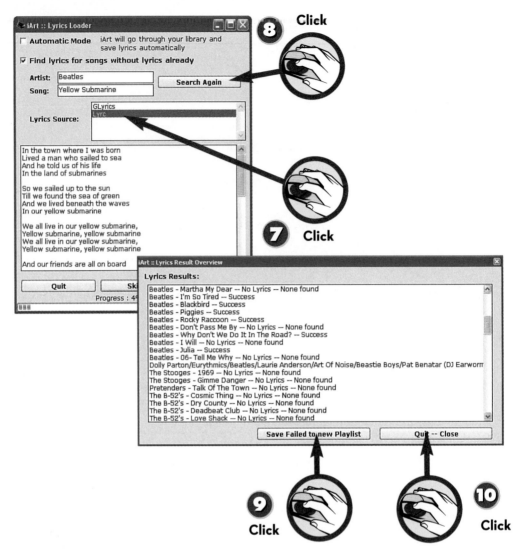

7 With Automatic Mode disabled, choose a different database from the **Lyric Source** list when lyrics don't appear in the lower window for a selected song.

8 Click **Search Again**.

9 Click **Save Failed to New Playlist**. This option might be useful if you want to search for lyrics from another source and add them manually.

10 iArt displays the results of your lyric search. Click **Quit – Close** to end your iArt session.

End

NOTE

Get Your Lyrics Here

Another option for grabbing iTunes lyrics is PhiloCode Solutions's MiniLyrics (free, www.philocode.com/minilyrics).

ADDING LYRICS TO iTUNES MANUALLY

You can manually add lyrics to iTunes by pasting or typing text into the Lyrics section of each song's Info window.

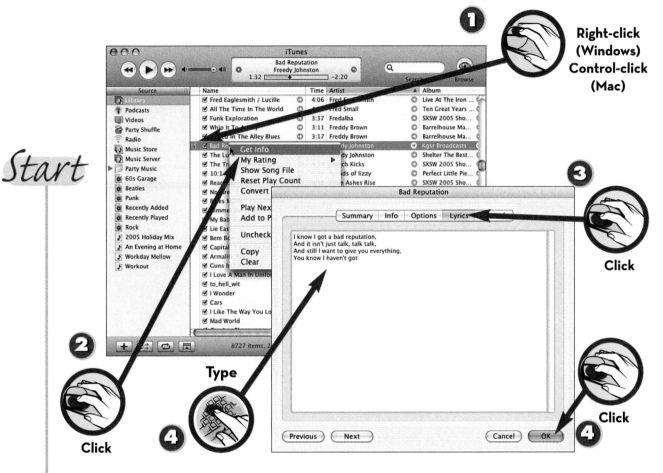

Start

Right-click (Windows) Control-click (Mac)

Click

Type

Click

Click

End

1. In iTunes, right-click (Windows) or Control-click (Mac) a song for which you know or have found the lyrics.

2. Select **Get Info** from the menu.

3. Click the **Lyrics** tab.

4. Type or paste the song's lyrics into the field. Click **OK**.

NOTE

Edit Existing Lyrics

Lyric databases don't always have the correct info. If you discover that lyrics you've downloaded are incorrect, open the song's Info window and edit the lyrics that appear there. Next time you retrieve lyrics automatically, be sure not to update lyrics you have edited by hand.

ADDING AND VIEWING LYRICS ON YOUR iPOD

After you have downloaded or manually entered lyrics for your songs in iTunes, you need to sync your iTunes library to the iPod. Then the lyrics appear under the Notes menu on your iPod.

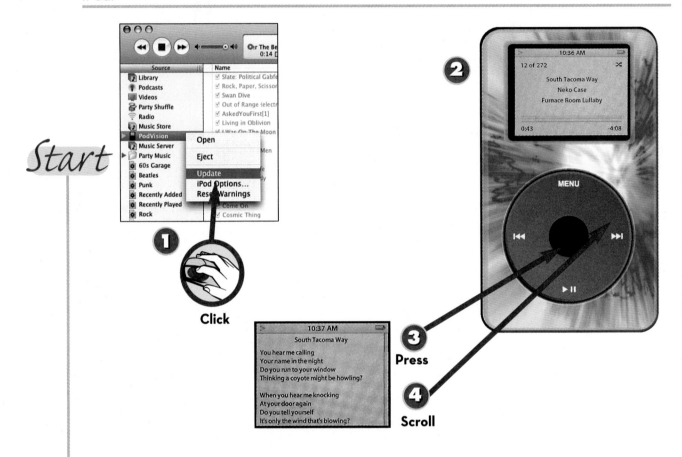

Start

Click

Press

Scroll

1. After adding lyrics, right-click (Windows) or Control-click (Mac) the **iPod** item and choose **Update** to sync to the library. Disconnect it when the update is complete.

2. On the iPod, play a song for which you have downloaded or typed lyrics.

3. Press the **center button** several times until you see the song's lyrics. The number of button presses required depends on whether the song has album art.

4. Use the click wheel to move through the lyrics.

End

TIP

Center Button Options

Pressing the center button while a song plays gives you different information, based on whether the track has album art or lyrics. The available modes are Play Status, Scrubber, Album Art, Lyrics/Description, and Rating.

ADDING PDFS TO iTUNES

iTunes can list PDF files in the music library. You can even associate them with an album, as in the case of liner notes or guitar tablature for the album.

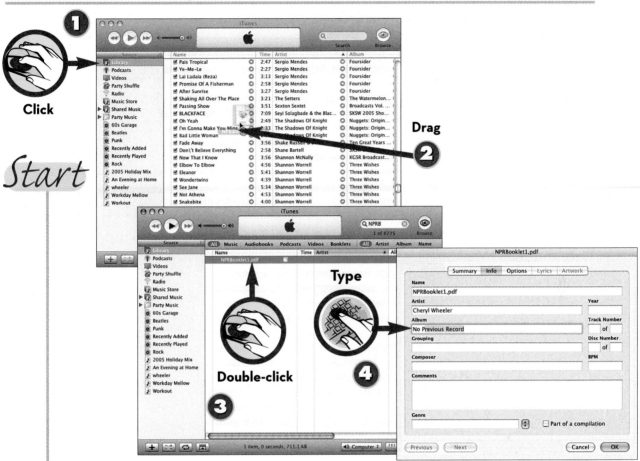

Click

Start

Drag

Type

Double-click

1 Select **Library** or a playlist in iTunes.

2 Locate a PDF file you want to add to iTunes and drag the file into the content pane.

3 Double-click the PDF file in iTunes to open it. The file opens in Adobe Reader on a Windows computer and in Preview on a Mac.

4 To associate a PDF with an album, open the Info window for the PDF file and change the album name to that of the album to which the file belongs.

End

NOTE
More Ways to Get PDFs

Some albums available at the iTunes Music Store include PDF files, as does the U2 music collection bundled with the special edition U2 iPod. Podcasters might also send a PDF file via iTunes, as the iLounge iPod news site did in late 2005.

ADDING ARTWORK TO iTUNES TRACKS

Songs you download from the iTunes Music Store, as well as many podcasts, include artwork you can view in iTunes and on color iPods. You can add artwork to tracks you've ripped from CDs or that you have acquired from other sources.

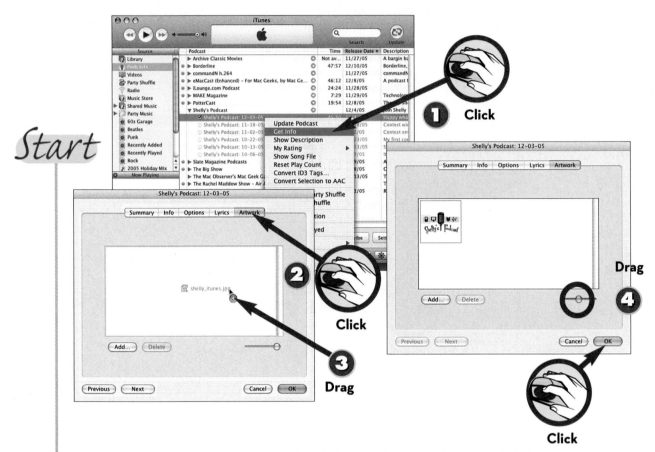

Start

1. With a song selected in iTunes, right-click (Windows) or Control-click (Mac) and choose **Get Info** to open the Info window.

2. Click the **Artwork** tab.

3. Drag a JPEG, GIF, TIFF, or other image file from the Finder (Mac) or Windows Explorer (Windows) into the artwork pane.

4. Drag the slider to change the size of the image in the window, and click **OK** to finish editing the artwork.

Continued

NOTE

iPod Artwork

Artwork for any iTunes track displays on your iPod when the track is playing. To see a close-up of the artwork, press the **center button** twice. After a few seconds, the display returns to normal.

TIP

Downloading Artwork

Like lyrics, artwork can be downloaded from the Internet into iTunes. Export Artwork ($9.95 shareware, www.dizzypenguin.com/automac-it/) is a Mac option. Windows users can download artwork with iArt, which also downloads lyrics.

Click — Double-click

5 Click the **Show/Hide Artwork** button to open the artwork pane.

6 Double-click the track to which you've added artwork.

7 The art appears in the artwork pane.

End

TIP
Drag in Some Art
To add artwork to a song that is currently playing in iTunes, drag an image into the artwork pane as the song plays.

TIP
Art for All
To add the same piece of artwork to all songs on an album, select all of the songs and then drag the artwork into the artwork pane.

BURNING DISCS WITH iTUNES

iTunes is both an input and an output application. That means that besides ripping CDs and importing files, you can burn your own CDs, either to play on a home or car stereo, or as backups for your computer-based music collection.

iTunes can burn standard audio CDs, MP3 CDs, data CDs, and data DVDs. You need a CD or DVD burner installed in or attached to your Mac or PC. To complete the tasks in this chapter, you also want to get a supply of blank CDs or DVDs that are compatible with your disc burner.

Different disc formats can be played in CD/DVD players that are compatible with the format you choose. For example, most CD players can play the audio CDs you burn with iTunes, but might not be able to play MP3 discs. So be sure that the format you use will work with the player you have in mind.

To comply with U.S. copyright laws, discs you burn with iTunes must be for personal use only and can't include copyrighted material you do not own.

DISC BURNING OPTIONS

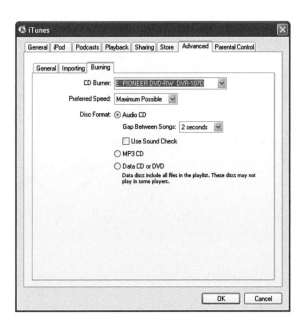

BURNING A PLAYLIST TO A CD OR DVD

The steps required to burn CDs or DVDs of different formats are very similar, whether you're burning an audio CD, MP3 CD, data CD, or data DVD.

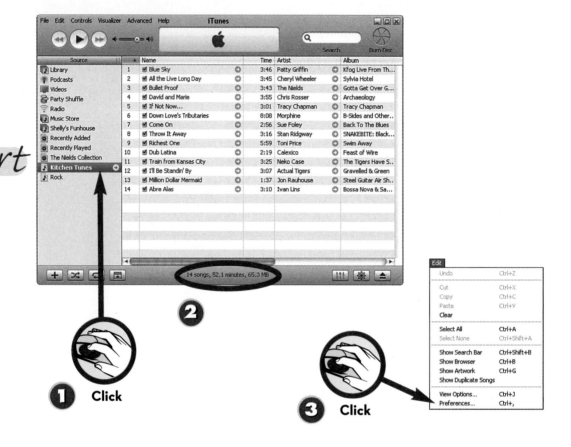

1 Select the playlist you want to burn.

2 In the Time/Capacity display, verify that the playlist will fit onto a single disc. (See the note at the bottom of this page for details.)

3 Open iTunes Preferences by choosing **Edit**, **Preferences** (Windows) or **iTunes**, **Preferences** (Mac).

Continued

NOTE

Disc Capacity

You can burn up to 700MB on a single data or MP3 CD. A DVD can hold up to 4.7GB of data. The capacity of an audio CD is not measured in megabytes, but in time; you have up to 80 minutes. Keep in mind that these numbers reflect the maximum amount of information or music you can cram onto a disc. You might get slightly less.

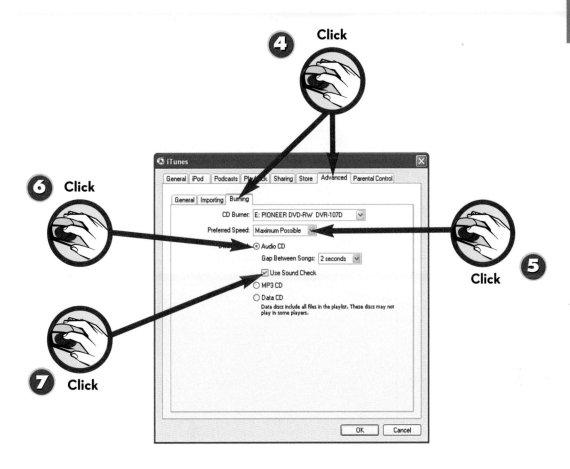

4 Click the **Advanced** tab, and then the **Burning** tab.

5 Choose an option from the **Preferred Speed** menu.

6 To burn an audio CD, choose **Audio CD** from the Disc Format list, and select a time from the **Gap Between Songs** menu (2 seconds is common).

7 Click the **Use Sound Check** check box to have iTunes match the sound levels of the items included on your playlist with one another.

Continued

TIP
Only MP3s on an MP3 CD
Music files in your library that are not MP3 files cannot be included on an MP3 CD. If you use a playlist containing non-MP3 files, iTunes displays an error message and lists the problem files. Use iTunes to convert the files into MP3s.

TIP
The Need for Speed
In step 5, **Maximum Speed** is the fastest way to burn a disc, but you might want to choose a slower speed if you have experienced errors while burning discs from the batch you are currently using.

Click 8

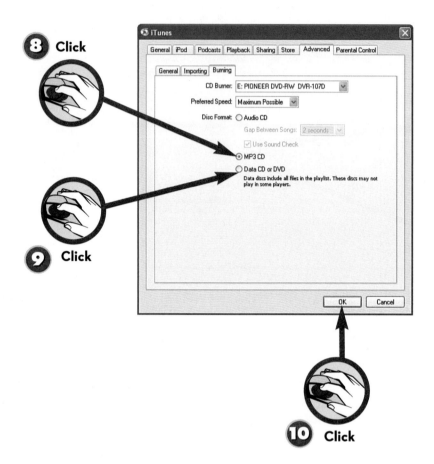

Click 9

Click 10

8 To burn an MP3 CD, click **MP3 CD**.

9 To burn a data CD, click **Data CD** or **DVD**.

10 Click **OK** to close iTunes's Preferences.

Continued

TIP
Data CDs and DVDs
A data CD or DVD is one that can be read by your computer just like any other type of removable media. You can copy its files to a hard drive, but data discs cannot be played in a CD player, or even on a computer, unless you first import files into iTunes or into another music-playing application.

NOTE
DVD Is Different
If your computer has a DVD recorder, the label in step 9 actually says Data CD or DVD. Click this to burn a DVD.

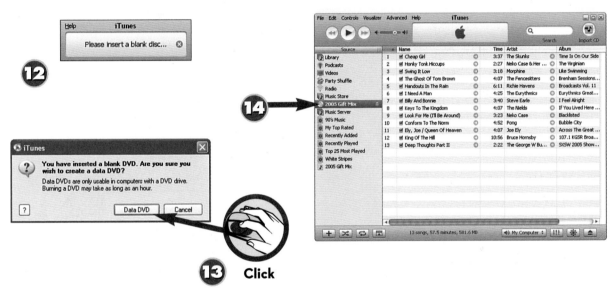

11 With the playlist selected, click **Burn Disc**, and then click it again.

12 Insert a blank CD or DVD when iTunes asks for one. iTunes verifies that the playlist will fit.

13 iTunes begins copying your files and burns the disc. If you're burning a DVD, iTunes reminds you that DVDs take awhile. Click **Data DVD** to proceed.

14 When the burn is finished, the new disc is selected in iTunes. Check to be sure that it contains the data you burned to it.

End

TIP

Limited Time

You can burn parts of a large smart playlist to disc without changing the playlist. Select the smart playlist and edit it by choosing Edit Smart Playlist from the contextual menu. Click the **Limit To** check box and type the number of tracks you want. Use the **Selected By** menu to control which songs are included in the smart playlist. When you've finished burning a reduced smart playlist, uncheck the **Limit To** check box to return the smart playlist to normal playback.

BURNING A MULTI-DISC PLAYLIST

When you try to burn a playlist that is too large to fit on a single disc, iTunes asks if you want to split the files among several discs.

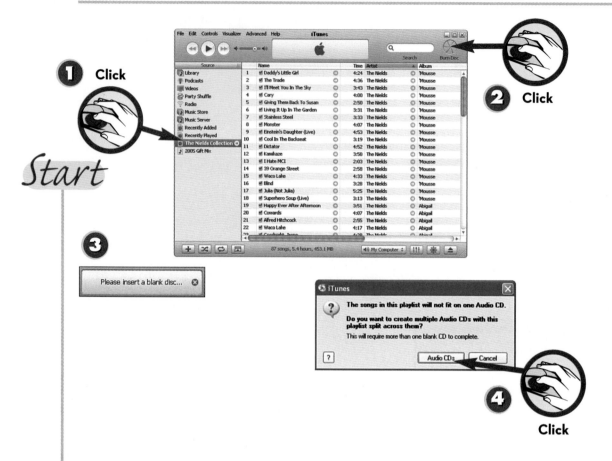

① Click

② Click

Start

③

Please insert a blank disc...

④ Click

① Select the playlist to burn and check the time/capacity to make an estimate of how many discs you'll need. Be sure the blank discs are nearby.

② Click **Burn Disc**.

③ iTunes calculates the number of discs you'll need, and then asks you to insert the first one.

④ iTunes warns that the playlist will not fit on a single disc. Click **Audio CDs** to proceed.

End

TIP
Refer to Prefs
If you expect to need multiple discs to burn a playlist to audio CD, but are not warned that you will need those discs, cancel the burn and check iTunes Burning Preferences to be sure that you've chosen Audio CD.

PRINTING A SONG OR ALBUM LIST

Song and album listings are intended to be printed on plain paper. You can even view album covers when printing an album list.

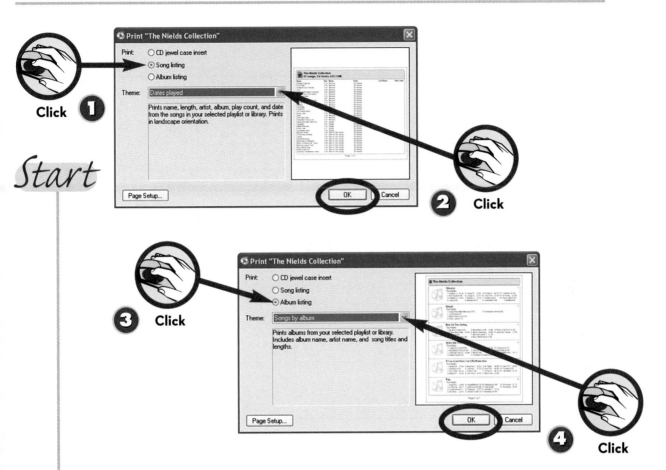

Start

1. Choose **File**, **Print**. Click **Song Listing** in the Print dialog box. A preview appears.

2. Choose a display option from the **Theme** listing. Click **OK** to print the song listing.

3. Click **Album Listing** in the Print dialog box to see a preview.

4. Choose a display option from the **Theme** listing. Click **OK** to print the album listing.

End

TIP
Larger Song and Album Listings
Although you are likely to print a CD jewel case for a single burned playlist, album listings and song listings are useful ways to get a printed record of your entire library or of a playlist you use in iTunes. You might want a song list of all the music you've purchased at the iTunes Music Store, for example. Just select the library or a playlist and click **File**, **Print**.

PRINTING DISC INSERTS

iTunes includes a printing feature that transfers the ID3 tags for a playlist onto CD inserts or song lists. ID3 tags contain the song name, artist, album, and other information about an audio file.

Start

Click

Type

Click

① Select a playlist for which you want to create a CD insert.

② Examine the **Name** and **Artist** ID3 tags for each track to be sure the text is what you want to see on the CD insert.

③ Correct any errors you find, using the track's Info window.

④ Choose **File, Print.**

Continued

NOTE

Not All ID3 Tags Are Covered

Many songs include lots of information in their ID3 tags; either by default or because you've added this information. Only the Name and Artist are included on printed CD inserts.

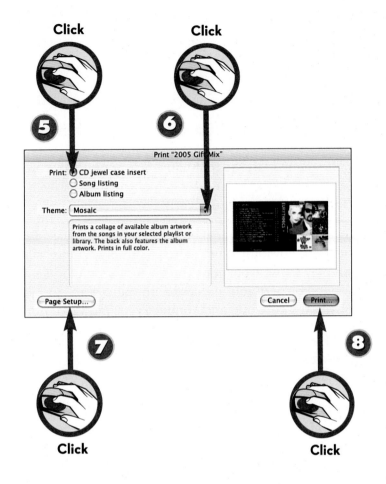

5 Click the **CD Jewel Case Insert** button to print one. A preview of the insert appears in the window.

6 Choose a display option from the **Theme** menu and notice the change in the preview area.

7 Click **Page Setup** and specify settings for your printer.

8 Click **Print**.

End

NOTE

More or Less Album Art

The number of album covers represented in a graphical CD insert depends upon how many of the tracks in your playlist have art. If the playlist is composed of songs you purchased from the Music Store and songs you ripped from CDs, you'll see art from the purchased items.

ADVANCED iPOD AND iTUNES

iTunes has many features that you won't necessarily run across in the course of your normal music listening. Each of them provides a way to get more from your iTunes listening experience.

Sharing an iTunes library makes your tunes available to other iTunes users on your network. Another way to share is to play iTunes tracks on your stereo. You can play music from your iTunes library on a home stereo system in three basic ways: connect your computer to the stereo, add your stereo system to your computer network, and connect your iPod to a home stereo system.

Give your eyes a break while you're listening to music with the iTunes visualizer. The visualizer is a screen saver for the iTunes window or for the entire screen.

Finally, if you're a Mac user, you have access to many great tools written in the AppleScript programming language. I'll show you how to find and install AppleScripts that add many extra features to iTunes.

iTUNES'S ADVANCED FEATURES

Shared libraries

Shared playlist

Airport Express menu

Visualizer on/off

SHARING YOUR iTUNES LIBRARY

If your computer is on a local network in your home or office, you can share your music library with other iTunes users.

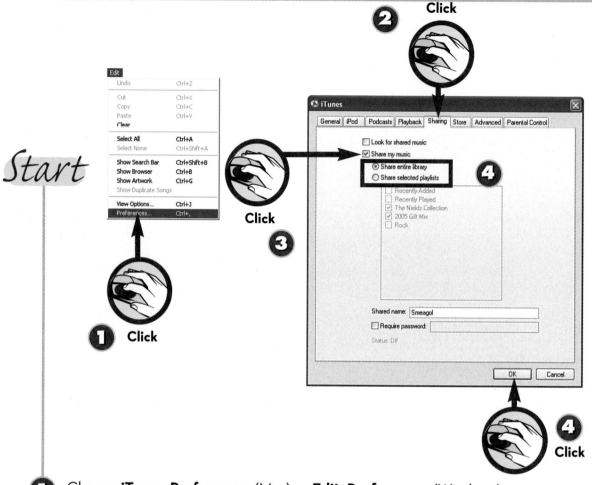

2 Click

Start

Click

3

1 Click

4

Click

1 Choose **iTunes**, **Preferences** (Mac) or **Edit**, **Preferences** (Windows).

2 Click the **Sharing** tab.

3 To share your iTunes library with others on your network, check the **Share My Music** check box.

4 You can share all of your music by clicking **Share Entire Library**, or limit what's shared by clicking **Share Selected Playlists**. Click **OK**.

Continued

TIP

Your Playlists Preserved

When you share your complete music library, all of your regular and smart playlists are visible to other iTunes users on your network. The built-in playlists, including Podcasts, Videos, Party Shuffle, and Radio, are not visible, but their contents, which are part of your music library, are available.

NOTE

Tres Amigos

Up to three users can be connected to your shared iTunes library at a time.

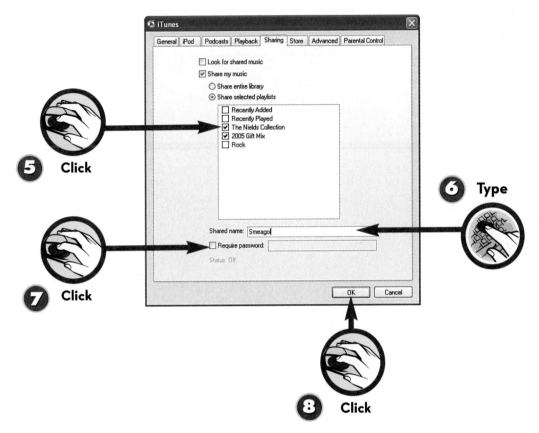

5 Click

6 Type

7 Click

8 Click

5 If you selected the **Share Selected Playlists** option, click the check boxes for each playlist you want to share.

6 Type a name for your shared library in the **Shared Name** field, or use the default name (based on your computer username).

7 To limit access to your shared music, click the **Require Password** check box and type the password.

8 Click **OK** to close iTunes Preferences. Your music is now available to other iTunes users on your network.

End

TIP

Where Do You Share?

When you share your laptop's iTunes library while traveling, it is visible to anyone using iTunes on the same network, including wireless networks in coffee shops, hotel networks, and so on. This won't increase your risk of viruses or other malicious attacks, but users connecting to your machine on a wireless network might slow down your network access. You can uncheck the **Share My Music** check box to temporarily disable music library sharing, or use the password feature to restrict access.

LISTENING TO MUSIC FROM A SHARED iTUNES LIBRARY

If another iTunes user on your local network has shared her music library, you can connect to it and play the contents on your computer.

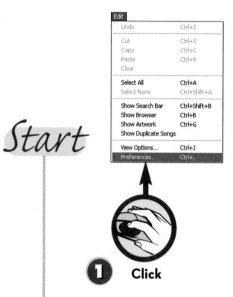

Start

1 Click

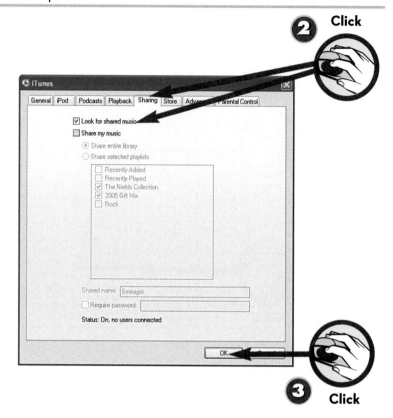

2 Click

3 Click

1 Open iTunes Preferences (choose **Edit, Preferences** for Windows users and **iTunes, Preferences** for Mac users).

2 Click the **Sharing** tab and check the **Look for Shared Music** check box.

3 Click **OK**.

Continued

TIP

You Can Listen, But You Can't Copy

Shared music you play on your computer cannot be copied to your iTunes library. You also cannot burn discs from a shared playlist. You can play shared music as long as the computer that contains it is connected to the network and has iTunes open.

TIP

Are You Authorized?

To play a song purchased from the iTunes Music Store, you must enter the ID used to purchase the song. Up to five computers on a network can be authorized to play music store purchases.

6 Click

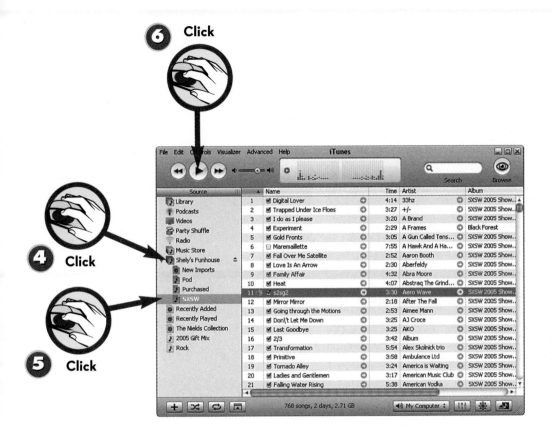

4 Click

5 Click

4 Click the shared playlist in the source pane.

5 If multiple playlists have been shared, click the expansion triangle to see them, and select the playlist you want to play.

6 Select a song and click **Play**. You can use the rest of iTunes's playback controls, along with most of the options on the Controls menu.

End

TIP

Multiple Servers

If several people on a network are sharing their iTunes libraries, you see a Shared Music item in the source pane. Click the expansion triangle next to it to see all of the currently shared iTunes libraries.

PLAYING YOUR ITUNES LIBRARY ON A STEREO SYSTEM

To play iTunes tracks on your home stereo system, you need a cable with two male RCA connectors on one end and a single male 1/8-inch connector on the other end. You can find these cables at electronics stores, including Radio Shack.

Start

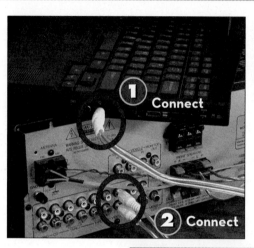

Press

Play song

1 With your computer set up near a stereo receiver, connect the 1/8-inch end of a Y-cable to your computer's headphone or audio-out port.

2 Connect the other end of the Y-cable to a pair of inputs on your stereo receiver. Many receivers have spare tape-in or video-in ports you can use for this purpose.

3 Activate the input you've selected by pressing the corresponding button on the receiver.

4 Launch iTunes and test your connection by playing a song. Adjust the volume on your receiver.

End

STREAMING MUSIC WIRELESSLY

A number of devices allow you to use a wireless network to send music from your iTunes library to your stereo system. I'll describe how to use Apple's Airport Express wireless access point. It works with both Mac and Windows computers.

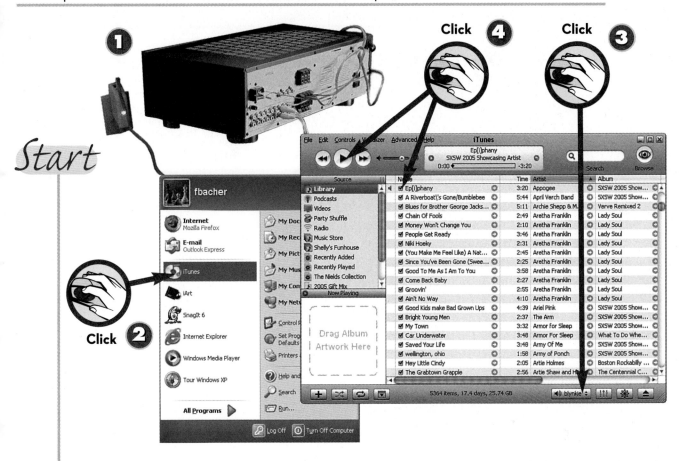

1 Set up the Airport Express according to the instructions provided with the unit. Connect the Airport Express to your stereo, using an RCA-to-1/8-inch Y-cable.

2 Launch iTunes on a computer that is connected to the same network as the Airport Express. The connection can be wired or wireless.

3 Choose the Airport Express base station from the menu in the lower-right corner of the iTunes window.

4 Select a song and click **Play** to hear the music on your stereo.

TIP

Other Ways to Go Wireless

Several companies sell devices that can stream your iTunes library to a stereo system. They include Macsense's HomePod ($249, www.macsense.com) and Squeezebox from Slim Devices ($249 and up, www.slimdevices.com).

iPOD MAINTENANCE AND TROUBLESHOOTING

Keeping your iPod running smoothly doesn't require much work because iPods are generally very reliable. You can do a few things to keep your iPod in tip-top condition and to solve problems when and if trouble strikes.

The most important things you can do to keep your iPod running right is to use the most up-to-date software and to take good care of the battery. You can also use the same disk management tools you use to keep your computer's hard drive running smoothly.

When trouble does strike, it's a good idea to diagnose the problem before panicking or throwing your iPod in the trash. A few quick troubleshooting steps can save you lots of time and money.

iPOD TROUBLESHOOTING STEPS

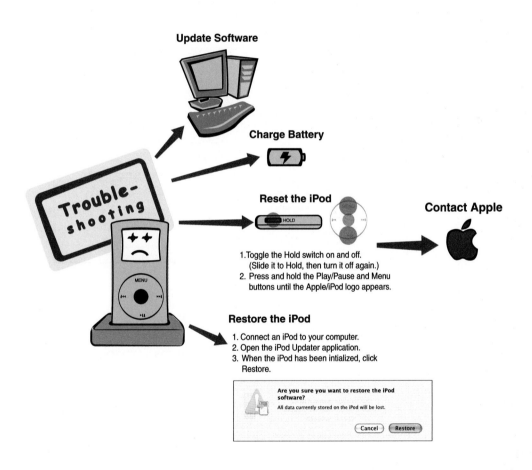

Update Software

Charge Battery

Reset the iPod

HOLD

Contact Apple

1. Toggle the Hold switch on and off.
   (Slide it to Hold, then turn it off again.)
2. Press and hold the Play/Pause and Menu
   buttons until the Apple/iPod logo appears.

Restore the iPod

1. Connect an iPod to your computer.
2. Open the iPod Updater application.
3. When the iPod has been intialized, click
   Restore.

Are you sure you want to restore the iPod
software?

All data currently stored on the iPod will be lost.

Cancel   Restore

Trouble-
shooting

MENU

KEEPING YOUR iPOD UP-TO-DATE

If your iPod is behaving strangely or if you can't find a feature or menu that should be there, you should check to see that your iPod's software is up-to-date. You can also check Apple's site for updates periodically, even when nothing is wrong.

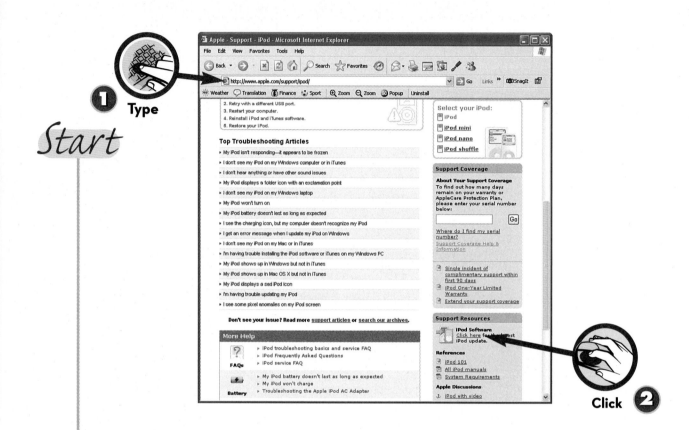

Start

Type

Click ②

1. In a Web browser, go to **www.apple.com/support/ipod**.

2. Click the **iPod Software** link under Support Resources. You might need to scroll to reach the link. Note that the wording or location of the link is subject to change.

Continued

-TIP-
Mac OS X Auto Update

The Software Update feature built into Mac OS X alerts you when new iTunes software is available. You are notified of new iPod software if your Mac contains any older version of iPod software. To check for new software, choose **Apple menu**, **System Preferences**, **Software Update**, and then **Check Now**.

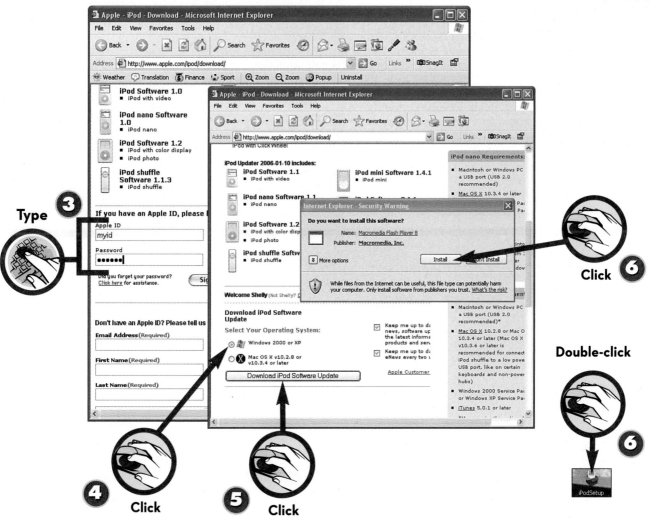

Type ③

Click ⑥

Double-click ⑥

④ **Click**

⑤ **Click**

③ Enter your Apple ID if you have one, and then your password. If you don't have an Apple ID, enter an email address, your name, and location.

④ Click **Mac OS X** or **Windows** to choose your operating system.

⑤ Click **Download iPod Software Update** to begin the download.

⑥ When the download is complete, double-click the iPod Updater installer and follow the wizard to install the update. Windows asks you to restart your computer; Mac OS X does not.

Continued

TIP
Check Your Version
To see what version of iPod software your player is using, choose **Settings**, **About** from the iPod's main menu. Compare this version number to the one listed on Apple's website to determine whether your device is up-to-date.

NOTE
Don't Email Me
If you don't want to receive email from Apple, uncheck the check boxes on the software updater page near where you log in.

210

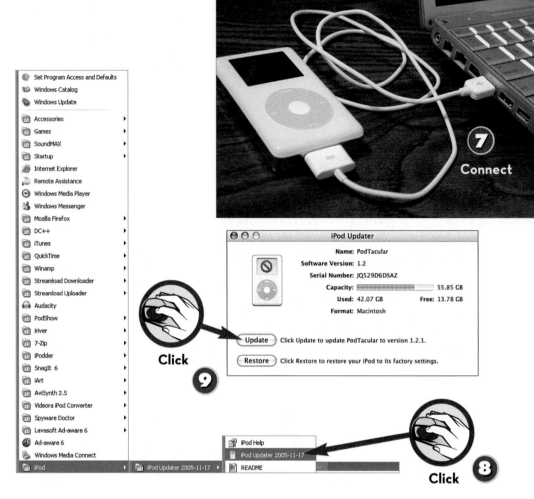

Connect

Click

iPod Updater

Name: PodTacular
Software Version: 1.2
Serial Number: JQ529D6DSAZ
Capacity: 55.85 GB
Used: 42.07 GB   Free: 13.78 GB
Format: Macintosh

Update   Click Update to update PodTacular to version 1.2.1.

Restore   Click Restore to restore your iPod to its factory settings.

iPod Help
iPod Updater 2005-11-17
README

Click

7 Connect an iPod to your computer after the installation is complete (and after restarting, if you're using Windows).

8 In Windows, choose **Start**, **iPod**, **iPod Updater**, **iPod Updater**. On a Mac, choose **Applications/Utilities/iPod Software Updater/iPod Updater**.

9 If your software is out of date, click **Update** to install the latest software. If your software is up-to-date, the Update button is dimmed.

End

 CAUTION

Careful with Restore

The iPod Updater application includes a Restore button. Restoring an iPod erases all data and returns it to factory default settings. Only use it if you have tried everything else, and if you have a full backup of your iPod's contents.

MAXIMIZING iPOD BATTERY LIFE

Each iPod model contains a rechargeable battery. You can improve your iPod's performance by minimizing excess battery use. Here are some suggestions for extending your iPod's battery life.

Start

Press

1

Press

2

Press

3

HOLD

1 When you remove your headphones to stop listening to music on your iPod, press **Play/Pause** to stop playback. To conserve the battery while away from your iPod, press and hold the **Play/Pause** button to put your iPod to sleep.

2 Move the **Hold** switch on the top of the iPod to the locked position to avoid accidentally activating the iPod by pressing buttons.

3 To turn off an iPod shuffle, move the switch on the rear of the shuffle to the **Off** position.

End

-TIP-

Disable Battery-Hungry Features

Set the backlight timer for the shortest amount of time with which you're comfortable. If the equalizer isn't on for a reason, turn it off. Keep frequent track changes to a minimum when your iPod's battery is low.

-CAUTION-

Don't Completely Discharge the Battery

Your iPod's lithium-ion battery does not need to be drained before you recharge it because it causes the battery to wear out more quickly. Completely discharge the battery, however, if you suspect battery problems.

KEEPING YOUR IPOD CHARGED

You can charge your iPod by connecting it to your computer or with an optional iPod AC adapter. Smart charging strategies can also help preserve your battery.

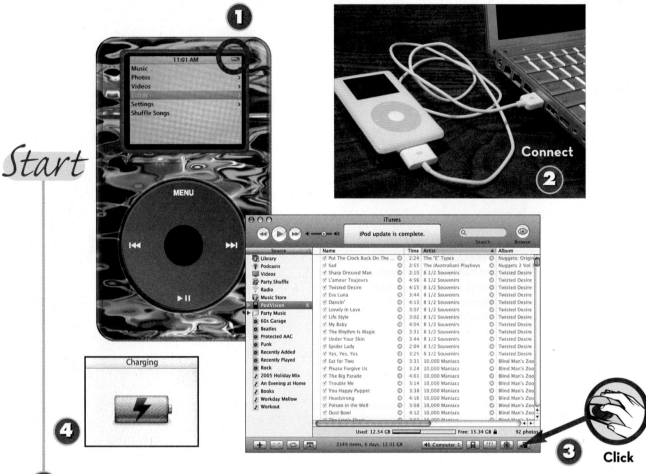

Start

Connect

Click

1 Check your iPod's battery indicator to determine whether the battery is low.

2 Connect the iPod to your computer or to an AC adapter. Leave it connected for three hours to fully charge the iPod.

3 If the iPod is connected to your computer, launch iTunes and click **Eject** to unmount the iPod. If the iPod is connected to an AC adapter, simply disconnect it.

4 The display indicates whether the iPod is fully charged or still charging. You can disconnect it at any time.

End

NOTE
Where's the AC Adapter?
Until recently Apple included an AC adapter with most iPod models. The adapter enabled you to plug an iPod into an AC outlet while away from your computer. You can still get an adapter from Apple for $29.95.

NOTE
Charge in Your Car
Several companies, including XtremeMac (www.xtrememac.com), Griffin (www.griffintechnology.com), and Belkin (www.belkin.com), offer car chargers. A car charger does not recharge your iPod as quickly as an AC charger or your computer.

RESETTING YOUR iPOD

When an iPod is not behaving as you expect it to—not responding or doing something it shouldn't when you press a button—a quick troubleshooting option is to reset it. Unlike restoring, resetting the iPod merely restarts it, rather than erasing data and settings.

Start

②

①

Press

① Press and hold the **center** and **Menu** buttons on the iPod until you see the Apple logo on the screen.

② To test the results of the reset, play a song and navigate through some of the iPod's menus.

End

TIP

Protecting the iPod

The iPod's chrome rear surfaces are extremely subject to scratching, even if you're careful. There are many kinds of iPod protection, generally fitting into three categories: shields, skins, and cases. An iPod shield, often made of a cellophane-like clear plastic, fits tightly around the iPod. A skin is more like a suit of clothes, while a case from be anything from an iPod wallet to a hard-shell box. See the Appendix, "iPod Accessories," for more information about all kinds of iPod protection.

RESTORING AN iPOD TO FACTORY DEFAULTS

You can completely erase your iPod's contents and return its settings to factory defaults by restoring the iPod. You might choose to do this if you have been having intermittent problems playing music, or if you want to associate the iPod with a new computer or music library.

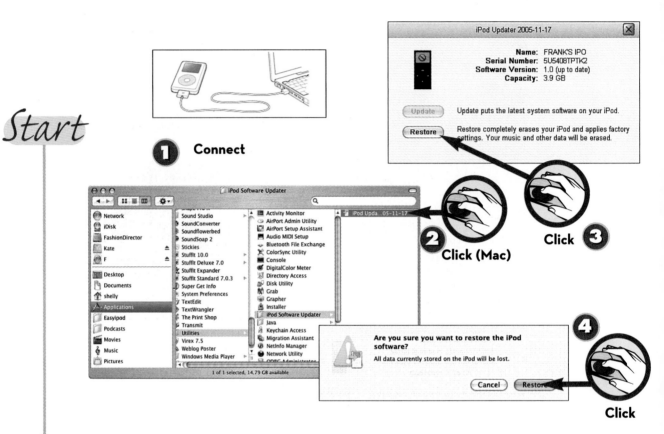

Start

1 Connect

2 Click (Mac)

3 Click

4 Click

1 Connect an iPod to your computer.

2 Open the iPod Updater application. It's in **Applications**, **Utilities**, **iPod Software Updater** (Mac) or **Start Menu**, **All Programs**, **iPod**, **iPod Updater** (Windows).

3 When the iPod has been initialized, click **Restore**.

4 Click **Restore** to confirm that you want to erase your iPod and reset it to factory defaults.

End

TIP

Multiple iPod Updaters

If you have updated your iPod several times, the iPod Software folder might contain multiple copies of the iPod Updater application. Be sure to use the file with the most recent date (it's in the file name). You might want to trash older versions of the updater.

iPOD TROUBLESHOOTING STEP-BY-STEP

Using the maintenance steps you've learned so far in this chapter, you can diagnose or eliminate most iPod problems.

Start

1 If you're having problems using your iPod, verify that it contains the most up-to-date version of Apple's iPod software.

2 Be sure that your iPod battery is charged.

Continued

TIP

Finding iPod Software Versions

Version information is available on the iPod: Choose **Settings**, **About** from the main menu to see the installed version of the iPod software. Another option: When you launch iPod Software Updater with the iPod connected to your computer, the software tells you whether your iPod is up-to-date.

Press

4

MENU

iTunes

iPod update is complete.

Search   Browse

Source	Name	Time	Artist	Album
Library	Put The Clock Back On The ...	2:24	The "E" Types	Nuggets: Origin
Podcasts	Sad	2:55	The (Australian) Playboys	Nuggets 2 Vol 3
Videos	Sharp Dressed Man	2:10	8 1/2 Souvenirs	Twisted Desire
Party Shuffle	L'amour Toujours	4:56	8 1/2 Souvenirs	Twisted Desire
Radio	Twisted Desire	4:15	8 1/2 Souvenirs	Twisted Desire
Music Store	Eva Luna	3:44	8 1/2 Souvenirs	Twisted Desire
PodVision	Dancin'	4:13	8 1/2 Souvenirs	Twisted Desire
Party Music	Lonely In Love	3:07	8 1/2 Souvenirs	Twisted Desire
60s Garage	Life Style	3:02	8 1/2 Souvenirs	Twisted Desire
Beatles	My Baby	4:04	8 1/2 Souvenirs	Twisted Desire
Protected AAC	The Rhythm Is Magic	3:31	8 1/2 Souvenirs	Twisted Desire
Punk	Under Your Skin	3:44	8 1/2 Souvenirs	Twisted Desire
Recently Added	Spider Lady	2:04	8 1/2 Souvenirs	Twisted Desire
Recently Played	Yes, Yes, Yes	3:25	8 1/2 Souvenirs	Twisted Desire
Rock	Eat for Two	3:31	10,000 Maniacs	Blind Man's Zoo
2005 Holiday Mix	Please Forgive Us	3:24	10,000 Maniacs	Blind Man's Zoo
An Evening at Home	The Big Parade	4:01	10,000 Maniacs	Blind Man's Zoo
Books	Trouble Me	3:14	10,000 Maniacs	Blind Man's Zoo
Workday Mellow	You Happy Puppet	3:38	10,000 Maniacs	Blind Man's Zoo
Workout	Headstrong	4:16	10,000 Maniacs	Blind Man's Zoo
	Poison in the Well	3:08	10,000 Maniacs	Blind Man's Zoo
	Dust Bowl	4:12	10,000 Maniacs	Blind Man's Zoo
	The Lion's Share	3:03	10,000 Maniacs	Blind Man's Zoo

Used: 12.54 GB   Free: 15.34 GB   92 photos

2349 items, 6 days, 12.01 GB   Computer

Click   **3**

3 If you cannot charge the iPod, connect it to your computer or an AC adapter, and unmount it by clicking the **Eject** button in iTunes. Now you can use the iPod.

4 Reboot your iPod by resetting it (press the **center** and **Menu** buttons simultaneously).

Continued

Trouble-
shooting

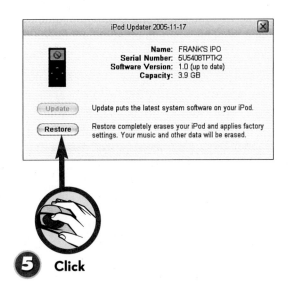

5 Click

5 Restore your iPod to its factory default settings. This erases all data.

6 If you still can't get the iPod to work or hold a charge, contact Apple or take your iPod to an Apple store.

End

TIP

AppleCare for iPods

Each iPod comes with a one-year warranty. You can purchase additional years of warranty protection when you buy an iPod at the Apple Store, or anytime within the initial free warranty period. Rates vary by iPod model.

iPOD ACCESSORIES

Steve Jobs calls it "the iPod economy"—the plethora of cases, gadgets, headphones, speakers, adapters, and other items available as accessories for your iPod. Whether or not it's reasonable to compare iPod stuff to an economy, it is true that a growing number of companies are creating or customizing items just for iPod users. Some are fun and frivolous; some make using or carrying the iPod much easier. In this appendix, you take a look at several kinds of accessories and a few examples from each category. This is by no means a comprehensive guide, but you'll get an idea of what's available, and maybe which ones you need (as opposed to those you just want very badly).

Cases and skins are among the most popular iPod accessories. You can cover your iPod with a protective layer, or simply add a tattoo, wrap, or even crystals to customize the iPod to your own distinctive taste. Throughout the chapters in this book are examples of various cases (from iSkin.com), wraps (from Designerskins.com), and even a crystal-studded iPod (from crystalicing.com). Take a look at what's available on these sites, as well as the multitude of others that are out there, before deciding on the accessory that is right for you.

BASIC ACCESSORIES FROM APPLE

Apple makes iPod accessories that range in price from $20–$40. Some of these were formerly included with iPods with displays, but are now sold separately. In addition to the items pictured here, you can buy docks specifically designed for the iPod nano and iPod shuffle, armbands, cases, a remote control/FM radio, and a camera adapter, each with the Apple brand. The Apple online and retail stores also feature accessories from other companies.

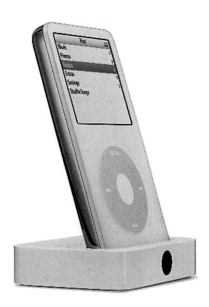

iPod Universal Dock

iPod USB Power Adapter

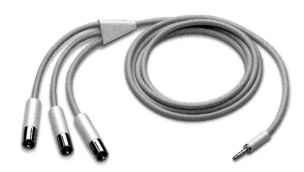

iPod AV Cable

SKINS AND CASES

You can buy two basic types of protection for your iPod: skins and cases. Within each category, you find a wide variety of options from many vendors. Some are designed to protect the iPod, while others emphasize fashion. An iPod skin is a tight-fitting cover, with openings for the display, controls, and connector ports. Shields are a variation on this idea. They consist of static film that adheres to the iPod and guards against scratches. Cases are larger protective containers made of leather, plastic, or metal, sometimes with a belt clip or lanyard. Some cases are padded and fashionable; others are sturdy, shock-resistant enclosures that can survive the elements. A few are waterproof.

The iPod nano and iPod shuffle require cases designed specifically for them because of their unique dimensions. As this book went to press, few cases designed specifically for the fifth-generation (video) iPod were available. The dimensions of the 5G iPod are the same as those of its predecessor, so it fits into older cases. The only drawback of this solution is that the edges of the 5G iPod's wide screen might be covered when you use an older-style case.

iSkin Vibes

iSkin eVo3

Belkin Carabiner case

Griffin iVault for the iPod shuffle

OtterBox iPod shuffle case

Belkin Folio case

SPEAKER SYSTEMS

The iPod was designed for use on the go, with headphones. A number of inventive vendors offer speaker systems, making it possible to share your tunes with the world and charge your iPod while you're at it. Most speaker systems are designed around the iPod's form factor, and connect to it via the dock connector or the iPod shuffle's USB port. Most also connect to AC power and charge the iPod while plugged in.

Griffin TuneBox

Bose SoundDock Digital Music System

Altec Lansing InMotion Plus

JBL On Stage II

AUTO ACCESSORIES

Your options for iPod auto accessories are varied. Because cars and auto stereo systems offer different kinds of connectivity, vendors offer a wide array of choices, ranging from FM transmitters and cassette adapters all the way up to custom head units with iPod interfaces.

The first decision you must make when choosing car accessories is what you want to do with your iPod while driving. The most basic items simply provide power to the iPod, allowing you to listen via headphones. Another group of devices transfers iPod audio to your car stereo. One step up from this approach you'll find devices that power the iPod and include an interface for controlling it. Audio interfaces that integrate into your car's head unit, or replace the head unit entirely, provide complete integration with your existing stereo system.

Griffin iTrip Auto

Griffin SmartDeck with Dock Connector

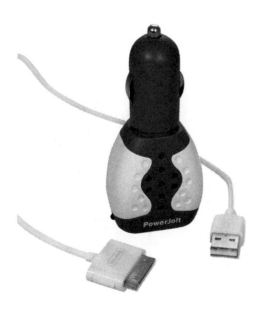

Griffin PowerJolt car charger

Griffin RoadTrip

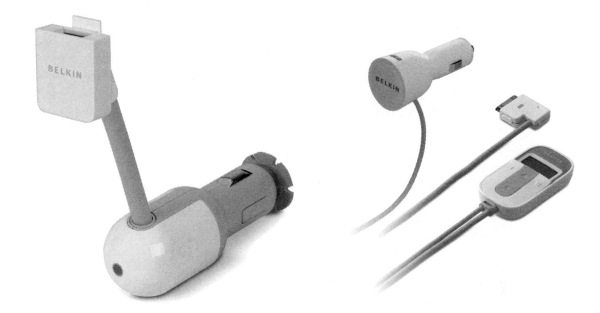

Belkin TuneBase for iPod shuffle　　　　　**Belkin TuneCast Auto**

Harman/Kardon Drive + Play

DOCKS AND STANDS

An iPod dock has two basic jobs: keep the iPod upright, and provide connectivity between it and other devices. A few companies make stands that don't have dock features. Speaker and audio systems that include docks you can use to support and charge your iPod have already been described, as well as Apple's universal dock, which supports all iPod models. Apple also sells docks specifically designed for the iPod nano and iPod shuffle.

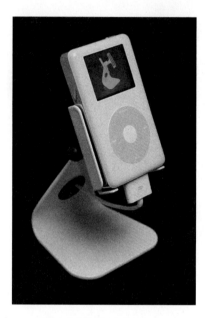

Thought Out Ped 2

Belkin Dock Adapter for iPod shuffle

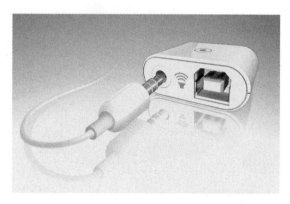

SendStation PocketDock Line Out USB

MISCELLANEOUS iPOD ACCESSORIES

If you need proof that the iPod is more than an MP3 player, take a look at the add-ons. Add an FM radio tuner, transfer photos directly from your digital camera to your iPod, or control the iPod with a wireless remote.

Griffin iFM radio tuner

Griffin AirClick wireless remote

Apple iPod Camera Connector

Belkin Media Reader

NUMBERS

1-click   iTunes Music Store account option that allows you to buy music without re-entering customer information already on file.

A

AAC (Advanced Audio coding)   A compressed audio format used by Apple to encode music files sold at the iTunes Music Store. AAC is also a good alternative to MP3 when ripping music in iTunes because it's slightly higher in quality.

AIFF (Audio Interchange File Format) Developed by Apple as the standard high-quality audio format on the Macintosh. AIFF is the Mac equivalent of the WAV format on Windows.

Airport Express   Apple wireless base station (access point) specifically designed to stream iTunes music to a home stereo system via a wireless network.

Apple ID   Customer ID used by the iTunes Music Store, the Apple Store, and Apple's registration system. You can use the same Apple ID for all transactions with Apple.

Apple Lossless format   A high-quality audio format that preserves the fidelity of native formats, including AIFF and WAV.

AppleScript   Programming language used to create custom commands and small programs on the Mac. AppleScripts are often highly integrated with Mac applications such as iTunes. Many AppleScripts have been developed to help iTunes users manage and re-organize their music.

artwork   An image that's associated with a song, podcast, or audiobook. The image appears when the artwork pane is open. You can also add artwork to files that don't have it. Artwork is copied to your iPod along with your audio files.

AV adapter   Cable used to connect an iPod to a television for viewing photos or video.

B

bit rate   The ratio of the number of bits transferred during a period of time, usually per second. Higher audio bit rates provide higher audio quality.

bookmarkable file   A file that can be stopped and restarted in iTunes or on the iPod without losing its previous play position. Audiobooks from audible.com and the iTunes Music Store are bookmarkable, as are podcasts you download via iTunes.

C

center button   Used to indicate selections on an iPod menu, or to switch display modes while the iPod is playing.

click wheel   Dial used to scroll through items on an iPod menu or to adjust iPod volume.

crossfade playback   iTunes setting that allows a song being played to blend into the next song.

D

dock adapter   Plastic holder that makes it possible to use any dock connector iPod with the Apple Universal iPod Dock. Dock adapters are shipped with the iPod nano.

dock connector   A 30-pin connector found on the bottom of all current iPod models, except the shuffle. Use the dock connector to connect an iPod to a dock or to your computer via USB. Most iPod accessories use the dock connector.

E

encoding   Converting an audio file to a new format or to a different bit rate and/or sample rate within the same audio format. When you rip a CD to MP3, you are encoding the resulting audio file in the MP3 format, using settings you choose in iTunes.

enhanced podcast   A podcast containing chapters. In iTunes, an enhanced podcast's chapter menu appears next to the search box, allowing you to choose one to play. When playing an enhanced podcast on an iPod, you can move from chapter to chapter with the Previous and Next buttons.

equalizer   iTunes and iPod feature for tweaking the sound of audio. The equalizer uses levers for several frequencies ranging from low to high. Adjusting the levers individually or using iTunes equalizer presets customizes the sound of different types of music.

F

FireWire   Known as IEEE 1394 in the Windows world but christened FireWire by Apple, this high-speed connector type was supported by all iPods prior to the release of the iPod nano. Neither the nano nor the fifth generation iPod supports FireWire for syncing. If you have a FireWire iPod cable and a computer with a FireWire connector, you can charge your newer iPod.

flash   A solid-state storage medium used in both the iPod nano and iPod shuffle. Flash storage is cheaper and more durable than hard disk storage.

G-H

gigabytes (GB)   One billion bytes.

Gracenote   An Internet database of songs, artists, and albums, formerly known as CDDB. iTunes contacts Gracenote each time a new CD or file is added. If it finds an entry for the item in the database, that information is downloaded to your iTunes library.

I-J-K

ID3 tags   Information identifying an audio file. ID3 tags include the name, artist, album, copyright date, and other information about a song, podcast, or other audio file.

iPod nano   The smallest iPod that includes a display. The flash-based iPod nano has most of the features (minus video support and recording capability) of the fifth-generation iPod. The iPod nano is available in white or black.

iPod shuffle   Flash-based, chewing gum pack–sized iPod player. The iPod shuffle has no screen and does not support playlists, but it functions in most other ways like a standard iPod.

iPod skin   Protective cover, usually tight fitting, for the iPod. Skins come in many colors and designs.

iTunes   Music playback and audio ripping software from Apple Computer. iTunes is pre-installed on all Macintosh computers. A Windows version is available for free from Apple. All iPod packages also include a copy. You can play most audio file formats, import CDs or audio files, and burn CDs or DVDs with iTunes. The software is also used to manage and synchronize all iPod models. iTunes includes podcast and video downloading tools and can play Internet radio streams.

iTunes browser   An iTunes feature that displays music by genre, artist, and album. When the browser is hidden, songs are displayed as a simple list.

iTunes Music Store   An Internet-based seller of music, audiobooks, and videos. The iTunes Music Store is integrated into the iTunes interface and controls a staggeringly high percentage of the online music market. The Music Store is perhaps best known for selling individual songs for $.99 in the United States and for similar prices in countries throughout Europe and Asia.

L-M-N

library   Central repository of all items tracked by iTunes. The library files contain pointers to each audio file, video file, and other files iTunes manages.

megabytes (MB)   Approximately one million bytes.

MP3 file format   The most popular format for compressed audio. MP3 files are small, making it easy to store many of them on an audio player such as the iPod. MP3 audio does not provide the high fidelity that AIFF and WAV files do, but many listeners feel that MP3's small footprint makes the compromise worth it.

O-P

On-the-Go playlist   Playlist you create on the iPod. Permanent playlists are created in iTunes and transferred to the iPod.

Party Shuffle playlist   Playlist that shuffles tracks from the music library or a playlist. Party Shuffle displays tracks that have been played and those that will be played in the near future. You can make changes to the play order within Party Shuffle.

Playlist   A means of organizing and playing audio files in iTunes and on the iPod. Playlists are used to keep similar types of files together, to sync files between iTunes and the iPod, and to provide special features for different kinds of media files. See also **Party Shuffle playlist**, **Podcasts playlist**, **Radio playlist**, **Smart playlist**, and **Videos playlist**.

podcast   Downloadable audio programs to which listeners subscribe. The iTunes Music Store provides a directory of podcasts, and iTunes itself includes a subscription feature that downloads new shows to your computer whenever they have been uploaded.

podcast feed   The URL that points to information about individual podcast episodes. This information tells iTunes when to download new shows and provides a description of the show.

Podcasts playlist   Special iTunes playlist that keeps podcasts organized by producer. The Podcasts playlist provides special settings for subscribing to and downloading podcast programs. Podcasts is also an iPod menu item that includes a list of all podcasts that have been synced from iTunes that include at least one podcast episode.

Preferences   An iTunes window where a wide variety of settings can be chosen. Preferences control the contents of the iTunes window, the way special playlists behave, how connected iPods are synced, when and how songs are imported, and more. To reach Preferences on a Mac, choose **iTunes, Preferences**. On a Windows computer, choose **Edit, Preferences**.

Q

QuickTime video   Apple-created video format that is commonly used to distribute video on the Internet. iTunes can play QuickTime movies.

R

Radio playlist   Special playlist containing listings of Internet radio stations. The list is provided by Apple and updated periodically.

ratings   Scale of one to five stars for picking favorite music in iTunes or on an iPod.

ripping   The common term for converting a CD into audio files on a computer. You can rip CDs with iTunes.

S-T

search bar   A way of narrowing search results in iTunes. When you search in your iTunes library or within the Music Store, the search bar enables you to choose results by type of content: music, podcasts, audiobooks, and so forth.

sharing   iTunes feature used to provide access to music on a local network.

show notes   Information about an individual episode of a podcast. Many podcasters include a rundown of the show, links to websites mentioned, and contact information for the host. Some podcasters include show notes within their podcast files, making the notes available when the show is played on an iPod.

shuffle   Play songs in a playlist or music library in random order.

Smart playlist   iTunes playlist you fill by creating criteria that tell iTunes which songs to add.

Sound Check   Volume normalization feature in iTunes and the iPod. Sound Check adjusts the volume of all tracks so they are played at approximately the same volume.

source pane   iTunes pane containing the music library, playlists, and a link to your iPod.

Standard playlist   iTunes playlist you create and fill manually by dragging items from the music library.

syncing   Copying iTunes files to your iPod or removing deleted items from the iPod. iTunes can sync your music library to an iPod if the iPod has enough free space, or you can tell iTunes to sync individual playlists to the iPod. Syncing also updates contacts and calendars stored on your iPod.

U-V

USB (Universal Serial Bus)   All current iPods can be connected to a Mac or PC using a USB port. USB 1 is an older, slower type of USB, while USB 2, recommended for use with an iPod, is much faster. All modern computers include USB ports. You can use either USB 1 or 2 with your iPod, but USB 2 is strongly recommended because it is much faster. iPod packages include a USB 2 dock connector.

Videos playlist   An iTunes playlist that can list or display preview images of videos that have been added to an iTunes library.

Visualizer   iTunes can display images, abstract images, text, or other visual elements as you play music. In addition to the built-in visualizer, you can download visualizer plug-ins from a number of websites.

W-X-Y-Z

WAV   WAVE form audio format, a standard high-quality audio format developed by Microsoft and IBM. iTunes and the iPod support WAV files.

Index

Index

fast forwarding/rewinding on iPods, 78

iPod shuffles, adding to, 60-61

iTunes playlists, adding/deleting from, 45

muting in iTunes, 71

playing in iTunes, 70

playing on iPods, 74-75

previous/next song, moving to in iPods, 78

previous/next song, moving to in iTunes, 70

removing versus deleting, 45

repeating in iTunes, 71

shuffling in iTunes, 71

shuffling on iPods, 80

skipping versus removing, 45

unchecking from playlists, 174

Sound Check feature, 87

speaker systems (iPods), 221

spyware, 180

stations (Radio playlists), 51

stereos, playing iTunes, 204-205

streaming music wirelessly, 205

synchronizing iPods, 16-17

syncing

definition/advantages of, 52

disconnecting after, 62

file repetition, 58

first time syncing, 54-55

manual iPod management, 56-57

overview, 59

photos. **See** photos

playlists to iPods, 58

T - U

televisions

photos from iPods, viewing on, 145

videos from iPods, viewing on, 116-117

text-based applications (iPods), 162

Thought Out Ped 2, 224

time (iPods), setting, 64-65

Time in Title option, 65

trailers. **See** videos

troubleshooting iPods, 215-217

unmounting iPods, 62

updating

iPods, 208-214

podcasts, 94-95

USB, 5-8

V

Videora iPod Converter, creating folders, 120

videos

adding to iPods, 112

bookmarking in iTunes, 111

downloading from Music Store, 108

DVD movies, converting, 121

iPods, playing on, 114-115

iTunes, 110-111

Macs, 118-119

managing, 113

Music Store, 109

QuickTime Pro alternatives, 118

Remember Play Position option (iPods), 114

storage capacities (iPods), 106

supported formats, 106, 118

televisions, playing on, 116-117

Windows PCs, 120-121

Videos Playlist menu (iPods), 113

viruses, 180

W - X - Y - Z

warranties (iPods), 217

WAV files, 23. **See also** audio files

244

Index

Windows PCs